William John Courthope

Ludibria Lunae

Or, the wars of the women and the gods, an allegorical burlesque

William John Courthope

Ludibria Lunae
Or, the wars of the women and the gods, an allegorical burlesque

ISBN/EAN: 9783337015893

Printed in Europe, USA, Canada, Australia, Japan

Cover: Foto ©ninafisch / pixelio.de

More available books at www.hansebooks.com

LUDIBRIA LUNÆ;

OR,

THE WARS

OF THE

WOMEN AND THE GODS.

An Allegorical Burlesque.

BY

WILLIAM JOHN COURTHOPE.

LONDON:
SMITH, ELDER AND CO., 15, WATERLOO PLACE.
1869.

[The right of Translation is reserved.]

TO

JOHN ADDINGTON SYMONDS,

IN TOKEN OF FRIENDSHIP,

AND

IN MEMORY OF MODENA,

I DEDICATE THESE PAGES.

CONTENTS.

	PAGE
Preface	vii
Book I.	1
Book II.	37
Book III.	69
Book IV.	105

"SENSATION, which means lively life, is the word of the epoch, and we say that the word, like the thing, so far from being vulgar, or wrong, or wicked, or distressing, is an excellent good characteristic of the wind and bottom of the period, and a pledge that we shall come to something or other remarkable before we lift these hounds of the hours and the days from their present full cry."—*Daily Telegraph, June,* 2, 1868.

> "Then we upon our world's last verge shall go,
> And view the ocean leaning on the sky;
> From thence our rolling neighbours we shall know,
> And on the lunar world securely pry."
> DRYDEN'S *Annus Mirabilis.*

"'Ἀλλὰ σὺ, ὦ φιλότης, μὴ πάθῃς αὐτὸ πρὸς ἐμὲ εἴ σε θησαυροὺς ἀνορύττοντα καὶ πετόμενον καὶ τίνας ἐννοίας ὑπερφυεῖς ἐννοοῦντα, καὶ τίνας ἐλπίδας ἀνεφίκτους ἐλπίζοντα, φίλος ὤν, οὐ περιεῖδον, διὰ παντὸς τοῦ βίου ὀνείρῳ, ἡδεῖ μὲν ἴσως, ἀτὰρ ὀνείρῳ γε, συνόντα, διαναστάντα δὲ ἀξιῶ πράττειν τι τῶν ἀναγκαίων, καὶ ὅ σε παραπέμψει ἐς τὸ λοιπὸν τοῦ βίου, τὰ κοινὰ ταῦτα φρονοῦντα· ἐπεὶ ὅ γε νῦν ἔπραττες καὶ ἐπενόεις, οὐδὲν τῶν Ἱπποκενταύρων καὶ Χιμαιρῶν καὶ Γοργόνων διαφέρει, καὶ ὅσα ἄλλα ὄνειροι, καὶ ποιηταὶ, καὶ γραφεῖς, ἐλεύθεροι ὄντες ἀναπλάττουσιν, οὔτε γενόμενα πώποτε, οὔτε γενέσθαι δυνάμενα· καὶ ὅμως ὁ πολὺς λεὼς πιστεύουσιν αὐτοῖς, καὶ κηλοῦνται, ὁρῶντες ἢ ἀκούοντες τὰ τοιαῦτα, διὰ τὸ ξένα καὶ ἀλλόκοτα εἶναι."—LUCIAN : *Hermotimus.*

PREFACE.

A WRITER, who adopts a prescribed form of poetry in a time when prescription of all sorts is regarded almost with prejudice, has no right to look for a very warm welcome from the public. No great powers of perception are required to understand that a pure revival of a classical style would be inadequate for the satisfaction of the present literary appetite. Power of any sort, however rough, at least commands respect, and the reader's intellectual vanity is delicately flattered with the sense of having deciphered what is obscure; but to recognize the plain usage of ruder times is to ignore the urbanity of culture, and not to be unmistakeably original shows a blindness to the mission of the modern Poet. Now, in a state of vigorous literary lawlessness, a writer such as I have spoken of must also be necessarily exposed to peculiar dangers from criticism. Even if he is fortunate enough to be praised, it often happens that he is credited by a friendly enthusiasm with intentions which he never entertained. If, on the other hand, he falls into the tender hands of a professor of æsthetics, he is not unlikely to be condemned upon abstract principles of poetry, which are generally the more positively asserted the more they diverge from poetical practice. A judge of a conservative disposition will very probably select some favourite poem as the measure of right and wrong in the particular style. In a time of undoubted cultivation it is impossible not to feel some regret that, owing to the rather revolutionary principles of our poetry, and the consequent difficulty of defining its liberties by the laws of Form, the critic should be frequently completely in the dark as to the motives of the author.

I hope, therefore, I may, without being accused of overstepping my functions, show as briefly as possible, by reference to precedent, what I consider to be the laws and limits of Burlesque. The first poem, that occurs to the mind as an example of the burlesque style, is the *Rape of the Lock*, and it would be impertinent for me to bestow a word of praise on so great a poem, even in a time which piques itself on having surpassed the best works of Queen Anne's era. I will only say, for my own purposes, that the method by which Pope has produced such a result is Paradox; by which I mean the quality that excites the fancy through the representation of events and persons either not existent in, or exhibited in a manner contrary to, the general order of nature. It is needless for me to point out how all the most trivial occurrences of life are elevated into fictitious dignity in Pope's heroic style; how the fancy is pleased by the discovery of a new world and invisible ministers in human affairs. A large demand is made upon the reader's faith; but, the hypothesis granted, there is nothing in the poem which the severest logic could pronounce improbable.

The English reader is apt to imagine that the Rape of the Lock exemplifies all the laws of Burlesque. But there is another quality, not, indeed, found in this poem, but entering largely into the composition of other styles—Irony, which, being much more complex in its nature than Paradox, is much harder to define. It may, however, be described as the manner by which a poet produces a sense of the ridiculous without himself appearing to laugh; and which, therefore, is adapted to touch the more subtle feelings, by rapid transitions from the absurd to the graceful, the tender, or the pathetic. Laughter is but a mask of feeling, and he who can remove it will discover the features of Melancholy.

Paradox and Irony may be united in the same style. The union appears in its most perfect form in the plays of Aristophanes. The stage offers the happiest opportunities for Paradox, because the fancy readily accepts what is immediately presented to the senses: and when, therefore, we remember that the stage for which he wrote was that of Athens, we cannot be surprised that the brilliant genius of Aristophanes should have produced burlesques, which have never been equalled, and seldom approached. Paradox and Irony in his hands are made to act and react upon each other with perfect regularity. We welcome, as if they were the friends of our everyday life, the lovely floating choruses of his Clouds and his delicately chattering Birds.

We feel more strongly the tender grace and sweet irony of the song of the Hoopoe to the Nightingale after the buffoonery of Peisthetærus and Euelpides. And who has not perceived in his heart a strange mixture of laughing and crying on reading the address of the Birds to the Children of Men?—

" ἄγε δὴ φύσιν ἄνδρες ἀμαυρόβιοι, φύλλων γενεᾷ προσόμοιοι, ὀλιγοδρανέες, πλάσματα πηλοῦ, σκιοειδέα φῦλ' ἀμενηνά, ἀπτῆνες ἐφημέριοι, ταλαοὶ βροτοί, ἀνέρες εἰκελόνειροι, πρόσχετε τὸν νοῦν τοῖς ἀθανάτοις ἡμῖν, τοῖς αἰὲν ἐοῦσι, τοῖς αἰθερίοις, τοῖσιν ἀγήρῳς, τοῖς ἄφθιτα μηδομένοισιν, ἵν' ἀκούσαντες πάντα παρ' ἡμῶν ὀρθῶς περὶ τῶν μετεώρων, φύσιν οἰωνῶν, γένεσίν τε θεῶν, ποταμῶν τ' Ἐρέβους τε Χάους τε, εἰδότες ὀρθῶς, παρ' ἐμοῦ Προδίκῳ κλάειν εἴπητε τὸ λοιπόν."

Irony has never reached so high a pitch. There is but one who can compare with the author of the *Birds*, and he is the author of the *Midsummer Night's Dream*. The words of Puck,—

" Lord, what fools these mortals be!"

which give the key-note of that play, might almost make us believe in the transmigration of souls—at any rate of the souls of poets.

But though Paradox and Irony have never been, and probably never will be, united so perfectly as in the genius of Aristophanes, there have been some who, in their own way, have made quite as remarkable use of Irony. The poetry of the Italians has peculiar advantages for the employment of this manner, on account of the sweetness of their language. Burlesque seems naturally to have taken firm hold on the Italian genius, from the times of their early sonnet-writers down to the period of *La Secchia Rapita*. I need only mention, however, the narrative styles of Ariosto and Tassoni, the masters respectively of the romantic and the serio-comic epic.

In the style of Ariosto the element of Paradox is quite subordinate. It is, indeed, true that the *Orlando Furioso* abounds in persons and things which are not met with in the world. Wizards, harpies, hippogriffs, goblins, and fabulous fish, appear and play their part with as much dash and spirit as the knights themselves. But these are the children of Turpin, not of Ariosto; and the latter, instead of surrendering himself, like Aristophanes, to the enjoyment of his own Paradox, conceals a vein of banter under the grave polish of that musical stanza, in which he reproduces the marvels of the Archbishop's chronicle. Careless and prodigal, he does not attempt to make the creatures of his Paradox into mouthpieces for his allegory after the more artistic fashion of Aristophanes. His work is like a skein of many-coloured threads, each continuous yet constantly lost sight of,—flashing in and out, under and above, without entanglement, yet without a plan. Thus—to take one instance of loose construction—the hippogriff which carries Astolfo over the whole face of the earth, is put into a stall when he reaches the Earthly Paradise, though the knight has still to perform his journey to the Moon, and might very well have been carried there on the back of so astonishing an animal. We are conveyed to the Moon with the Paladin and St. John in a chariot of fire; a supernatural vehicle, which of course affords the poet fresh opportunities of Irony, but which, being in itself superfluous, proportionately diminishes our belief in his Paradox. Yet, strange as it may seem, this studied negligence only intensifies the sense of Irony which we experience throughout Ariosto's wonderful poem. So grave is the style, so invariable the demureness, with which he changes his key from marvellous to real, heroic to base, coarse to fine, light to serious, absurd to pathetic, that even his disregard of unity seems only to increase the charm of his manner. The reader feels throughout that the poet is laughing at him, and acknowledges that, if Ariosto has less art and constructive power than Aristophanes, he has, if possible, even more play.

The same features are repeated in Tassoni, the inventor of the serio-comic epic, but they appear in him less clear and prominent, partly because of the more purely classical form of his poem, partly because his genius is of an altogether lighter calibre than that of the great poet of Ferrara. He has Pope's love of incongruity. The trivial subject of his poem, the Rape of the Bucket, which produced the great war between Modena and Bologna, gives fine scope for Paradox, the sense of which is heightened by the solemn deliberations of the gods. But he has also, what Pope has not, the genuine vein of Italian Irony. He frequently pauses in the midst of his comic narrative to mix the currents of feeling, by bringing in a serious stanza or a beautiful passage. On the other hand, his constructive talent is very inferior to that of Pope, and *La Secchia*

Rapita is little else than a brilliant succession of burlesque episodes.

Such are the models which I have had before my eyes. I am quite sensible that I have fallen very far short of the high mark which I proposed to myself: it is one thing to see the end, another to command the means. Still I have endeavoured to catch from the past some faint echoes of its noble music, and to combine them into a modern melody. My aim has been to reproduce, to the best of my ability, in the epic style, the allegorical spirit which pervades the dramas of Aristophanes, and it appeared to me that the best way of obtaining such a result was by uniting the classical method of Pope to the manner of the Italians. There is nothing inharmonious in such a coalition; nor have I at all departed from national precedent in looking to Italy for my models. Italian literature is the elder sister of the English, and the names of Chaucer, Spenser, and Byron, show how the instinct of our poets in all times has turned thither as the source of their inspiration. The taste of our time has no doubt been diverted into other channels. With the exception of Dante, the Italian classics are little read, yet I believe that, when clearness of intention and simplicity of style are once more properly valued, there will be no need for an English writer to dwell with more detail on the precedents of Italy than on those of his own country.

BOOK I.

ARGUMENT.

The World having now arrived at social perfection, Women alone are excluded from the Rights of Nature. Cornelia, a learned virgin, convokes a Woman's-Rights Convention, in which, after an exposition of the wrongs of the Sex, she proposes to lead a Colony to the Moon, and the immediate institution of a College to discover the art of Moon-flying and other lunar accomplishments. The proposal being joyfully accepted by the Assembly, the young and beautiful Celia objects to the exclusion of men, but is answered by Sibylla, the Prophetess of Progress, who denounces Love, and asserts the probability of new vital conditions in the Moon. The Assembly is ended with a solemn sacrifice to Progress. In the meantime Cornelia's winged Thought flies into the Moon, which at this period is in the possession of the Gods, who are represented as migrating thither after their expulsion from Olympus. The Moon is then described as an airless and silent solitude, the final abode (on the authority of Ariosto) of the foolish Thoughts of Man, which move day and night before the Gods over the Stage called the Paradise of Laughter. Cornelia's Thought, having arrived on the Stage, delivers her message to the Gods, and they, being cast into great terror, are addressed by Jove, and afterwards by Love, who undertakes an enterprise against the Women. The Book is concluded with the arming of Love and the laughter of the Gods.

BOOK I.

I.

OF wondrous worlds and Woman's wars,
I sing—how she, by Progress driven,
Raised high revolt, and when the bars
Of nature and old use were riven,
She mounted to the Moon and Stars,
And dared the silent Lords of Heaven.
Do thou, who didst behold these things,
Apollo, sound them on my strings.

II.

For when, by change of sun and shade,
Man's destinies, at length completed,
Had to perfection brought Free Trade;
When none by weight or measure cheated;
When each distinction, rank, and grade,
Was gone, and not a sewer was fetid;
When Capital was friends with Labour,
And like himself each loved his neighbour;

III.

When Catholics (and mice forsooth!)
Were starved with fasting from church tapers;
When Fancy, Liberty, and Youth,
Were schooled by Comte; when farthing Papers
Had fathomed every virtuous Truth
(Excepting how to kill the vapours);
When War and Murder were mere stories,
And younger sons were all grown Tories;

IV.

When Bubble-blowing had gone by,
Though Greenbacks ousted gold and copper;
When men in air like birds could fly,
And poets lived like the old Grasshopper; *
When laws of mental gravity
Proscribed all laughing as improper—
Woman, alone of biped wights,
Though perfect, still had nought but Rights.

V.

In either House, by sages backed,
She'd pleaded from the Law of Nature;
In vain; the Parliaments were packed;
And though a Liberal legislature

---

* Compare the account given by Plato, in the *Phædrus*, of the Golden Age of musicians and poets.

Had talked three Sessions of an Act
To add a cubit to man's stature,
They still denied the natural sequel,
That maids at least are free and equal.

VI.

All maids were wroth; but most of these
Cornelia, Poetess and Blue;
Whom far from mortal marriages
The Muses to their mount withdrew.
Like Pindar, at her birth their bees
From her young lips had sucked sweet dew,
Which, ne'er replenished from that hour,
Had left her smile extremely sour.

VII.

Light as a butterfly, she'd dipt
Through all the sciences erratic:
'Tis true the Asses' Bridge she'd skipt,
Yet was by nature mathematic
As Archimedes: she'd have whipt
Porson himself for faults in Attic:
And—so she did her sex eclipse—
Could argue in a fine ellipse.

VIII.

In poetry, by turns she graced
The shepherd's pipe, the lyre, the buskin;
And as for art, her trust she based
On the contemporary Ruskin;

She liked all schools, but found her taste
Most taken with the early Tuscan;
And had she known two notes apart,
She would have dis-composed Mozart.

IX.

True child of sweetness and of light,
She was all Art from top to toes:
Art made her beauteous tresses bright,
Art arched the crescent brows that rose
O'er spectacles, which, left and right,
Saddled a (modern) Roman nose.
Some said by Rachel's arts her years
Had been renewed, and some—her ears.

X.

Howe'er this be, there is no doubt
The wise Cornelia, brought to bay
By man's long tyranny, sent out
Swift petticoats one April day,
Bidding them town and country scout,
And scatter presents by the way,
Showing all people her intention
To hold a Woman's-Rights Convention.

XI.

With that—as when some town-lodged wight,
(Whose thrifty maid by chance remembers
To wake him for the season's sight,)
In the November of Novembers,

Starts up, and sees the Cave of Night
Blaze, fire-like, from its starry embers,
And countless meteors earthwards rolled
In curves of purple, green, and gold;

XII.

Or as some cat, discreet and wise,
But lean with crickets and long dearth,
Waits watchful, with half-open eyes,
At curfew, by the smouldering hearth;
And soon the furry tribes of mice
From countless holes creep forth on earth,
Ten thousand: Hope her breast inspires,
Crackles her fur, her fancy fires—

XIII.

So when, responsive to her call,
Matron and maid, with swift returns,
Come pouring from the counties all,
With joy Cornelia's bosom burns.
How empty now (she thinks) each ball!
How vainly sigh the queenless urns!
The empty cups she seems to see,
Bereaved of gossip and of tea.

XIV.

Besides, her fancy she regales
With thought that never twilight tatting
Shall please again the eyes of males,
Nor candles gleam on fair white satin;

For maids so many, ev'n in tales
Of lying poets, Greek or Latin,
Had ne'er been found with maids to agree
Since your good times, Penthesile.

XV.

Ah! did the maiden Muse not frown,
I'd bring my fancy's flower to fruit,
And paint you every various gown,
(Sweet language, eloquent though mute!)
Long trained, or circling like a crown
The ankle clipt in fairy boot;
The fairy boot the foot should show,
The bend above, the arch below.

XVI.

Then should you have before your eyes
White Arctic fox (thrice happy vermin,
That died to gain such paradise!)
Clasping their necks, or snowy ermine,
Smooth seal-skin in cross-fold, a prize
Snatched from the backs of diving mermen;
Fine shawls with India's soft-edged bloom,
And scarves bright-striped in Roman loom.

XVII.

Nor less the tiny bonnet fair
Should perch—as when a moth caresses
A primrose—midway in the hair,
Where scarce 'tis spied, and never presses:

Above, Martello-wise, in air,
Should rise a tower of alien tresses;
And many a head should woo the zone
With long love-ringlet—not its own.*

XVIII.

This Herrick might have done, not I;
Yet do I know the fresh spring weather
Laughed with more sunlight to espy
So many pretty maids together;
The birds sang in a bluer sky,
The thistledown and floating feather
Came round their waists, and played coquettes
With pencil-beaux and vinaigrettes.

XIX.

To see them meet, retire, advance,
A sea of gowns in ebb and flow,
It might have been a virgin dance,
Or—since the most were white as snow—
As in an orchard, if by chance
The fresh spring winds the branches blow,
And blossoms, delicate and pale,
Bow every petal to the gale;

---

* The idea of the chignon seems taken from Virgil's description of grafting,—

"Ingens
Exiit ad cœlum ramis felicibus arbos,
Miraturque novas frondes et non sua poma."
VIRG.: *Georg.* 2, 80.

XX.

Or, as the Moors with hammers dark
Twice beat the bell in Venice Square,
Then the white pigeons of St. Mark,
All snow and sunshine, pair by pair,
Curve to the window in an arc,
To take their old appointed fare
Of finest meal—a sight more pretty
Graces no European city;

XXI.

Such was the host: but as some daw,
Grey-pated, blown by many gales,—
Whom Starlings rank in reverent awe
With Nestor for long-winded tales,—
Hops on the steeple with a caw,
And o'er his chattering friends prevails;
So now, on platform high preferred,
Cornelia's queenly voice is heard.

XXII.

"Daughters of Eve! best known by this,
Her daughters, as most prone to dare,
Still to attempt our province is,
And then persuade mankind to share:
If woman, in the hope of bliss,
Was first to fall, it is but fair,
Now we behold a certain prize,
Our sex should be the first to rise.

XXIII.

"And us high courage more befits,
　Ground as we are by tyrants hard,
For all that's won by woman's wits
　As their monopolies men guard:
In Parliament no virgin sits,
　From pulpit, wig, and gown debarr'd!*
Forsooth! 'tis portion of our curse,
To wed, have babies, cook, and nurse.

XXIV.

"When thus oppressed in days of old,
　We read 'twas always woman's habit
To found far colonies, and hold
　Waste islands with the gull and rabbit: †

---

* It is rather amusing to compare the opinion of Tiresias (who had once himself been a woman) with the aspirations of modern ladies. Menippus asks him whether the life of men or women is preferable. Tiresias replies:—

"Παραπολύ, ὦ Μένιππε, ὁ γυναικεῖος, ἀπραγμονέστερος γάρ· καὶ δεσπόζουσι τῶν ἀνδρῶν αἱ γυναῖκες, καὶ οὔτε πολεμεῖν ἀνάγκη αὐταῖς, οὔτε παρ' ἐπαλξιν ἰστάναι, οὔτ' ἐν ἐκκλησίᾳ διαφέρεσθαι, οὔτ' ἐν δικαστηρίοις ἐξετάζεσθαι "—

("The Woman's, Menippus, much; for it is a comparative holiday. And the men are henpecked by the women; nor are the latter obliged to go into the army, or to become Volunteers, to talk in the House, or to be called on juries.")—LUCIAN: *Dialogi Inferorum*, 28.

† See *Orlando Furioso*, C. xxvii., for an account of the Settlement of the Amazons, its origin, and customs.

Maids nowadays are no less bold ;
But, ah ! there is no land to inhabit !
Each mid-sea rock maintains its man ;
Yet for brave hearts I've still a plan.

XXV.

" There is a Continent of Light,
Ample, but tenantless,—for now
The Man, the Bush, the Lanthorn bright,
For hill and valley, all allow,— .
A region that no mortal wight
Has reached, save that adventurous Cow,
Who, when the Dish purloined the Spoon,
Leapt over it—I mean the Moon.

XXVI.

" Hither with me mount those who dare :
Yet first upon our perils think :
How, when we've passed the outer air,
To gulfs of Nothing we may sink ;
Or we may find, once safely there,
We cannot breathe, nor eat, nor drink ;
For there's no water, as I'm told,
Nor air on that side we behold.

XXVII.

" But Hope supports my breast : I hear
From sages, whom to doubt were treason,
That in the other hemisphere
There's air ; at least, there is no reason

To show there's not; and so 'tis clear.*
To these fair shores, in my good season,
I mean from slavery safe to fly;
If not, at least free woman die.

---

* "The illustrious Hansen has held that it is quite possible that the Lunarians, on the side away from us, may have both water and an atmosphere."—*The Heavens:* A. GUILLEMIN, p. 159.

Here is a sample of Transatlantic eloquence which will show that woman is making satisfactory progress in the Christian virtues of Faith and Hope :—

"Hope, smiling seraph! beacon-light of every benighted mind; the rose that tinges every darkening cloud; the mountain rock for every incautious foothold; the shelter from every portentous storm! Its cheering beams penetrate the miseries of life, and flood the soul with the rapture of gladdening anticipations.

"To Man. If you lack faith in woman, review her history; study it heartily, seriously; take no bird's-eye glance, no slight plunge into the abyss of the past. Scan the motives upon which her conduct has ever been based. How can you fail to believe in her? And from the past deduce the future. Woman, like yourself, has in her a mystery of undeveloped power, living sources of thought. Her mission, it will dawn upon you in the fulness of light. You will believe her worthy to be your equal, and you will love to believe.

"Do what is right! For the day-dawn is breaking,
   Hailing a future of Freedom and Light;
Angels above you are silent notes taking
   Of every action! Do what is right.

"Do what is right! The shackles are falling,
   Chains of the bondmen no longer are bright,
Lightened by hope, soon they'll cease to be galling;
   Truth goeth onward! Do what is right.

"Do what is right! Let the consequence follow;
   Battle for Freedom in spirit and might;
And with stout hearts look ye forth to the morrow;
   God will protect you in doing what's right."

—*Speech of Mrs. Coe, of Ohio,
in the Second National Woman's-Rights Convention.*

XXVIII.

" But first one riddle we must read,
   Ere from this sphere we take our flight.
'Tis long since men of modern breed
   Traversed with wings the airy height,
And, passing swallows at full speed,
   Outsoared the daring Eagle's sight;
Yet still one secret from our race
Is hidden—how to float in space.

XXIX.

" So, since our flesh by nature clings
   To earth, and from dark sciences
We must invent moon-flying wings,
   A Gothic Hall I've hired on lease,
Where every maid who hopes high things
   Must graduate in high degrees;
'Twixt Oxford reared, a modern growth,
And Granta, soon to eclipse them both.

XXX.

" Hither, to teach us arts, shall come
   Professors from Lagado rare,
Who soar through Spiritland with Home,
   Or Zadkiel's Almanacks prepare;
Laws of perpetual motion some
   Shall show us, some the circle square,
Close space in two straight lines, and strive
To prove that two and two make five.

XXXI.

" Here, too, from Physics we must learn
To make our bodies light as dreams;
Here frame a Code of Morals stern,
Such as the lunar world beseems.
Truth's naked self we shall discern
In systems, and such soaring schemes
As by the merry Greeks were sung,
And are performed by Brigham Young.

XXXII.

" Then when, in abstract problems versed,
We've learned our senses to perplex,
We'll mount at once and dare the worst;
For if good Fortune save our necks,
Two worthy ends we gain—the first,
Destruction to the hated sex,*

---

* I cannot illustrate Cornelia's feeling better than by the pretty poetry of Miss Abby K. Price, read in the first National Woman's-Rights Convention,—

"Wait, boastful man! Tho' worthy are
    Thy deeds when thou art true,
Things worthier still and holier far
    Our Sisters yet will do.
For this the worth of woman shows,
    On every peopled shore,—
That still as man in wisdom grows
    He honours her much more.

" Oh, not for wealth, or fame, or power,
    Hath man's meek angel striven,
But, silent as the growing flower,
    To make of earth a heaven!
                                              [" Soon

Their wives being gone; for ours a fame
Beyond great Orontea's name."*

XXXIII.

She said.   With shouts her friends reply,
And swear against mankind alliance:
Some lift stilettoes to the sky,
Some with their bodkins hurl defiance,
And one (who squinted) vowed to die
Chaste as Lucrece for abstract science.
Such salves are found for spinsters' smarts
Moonshine and Bachelors of Arts!

XXXIV.

The echoes still roused wood and hill
When Celia followed,—Celia, queen
Of blondes, Venetian-haired, but still
With eyes like sloes, who, scarce eighteen,
And oft in Lancers, or quadrille,
Or livelier galop, lightest seen,
In sudden whim had sought retreat
And wisdom at Cornelia's feet.

" Soon in her garden of the Sun,
   Heaven's brightest rose shall bloom,
For woman's best is unbegun,
   Her advent yet to come."

* Orontea was Queen of the Cretan Amazons, described by Ariosto.

XXXV.

"Though wise the plan," she said, "and soon
  To be performed, in part you stray;
For if no men into the Moon
We take, we too must die as they.
A mortal husband for no boon
  Would Celia honour or obey;
Yet, sure, the woman's but a fool
Who would not wish for things to rule.

XXXVI.

"Slave though I be, yet, as coquette,
  'Tis sweet to make our tyrants chafe;
Victories behind the fan to get;
To be so rude and yet so safe;
To trample on a baronet;
  To treat a marquis as a waif;
And, O ye Gods, excuse my faults!
I own that I adore a waltz!

XXXVII.

"Besides, who knows what spectral host
  The Moon may breed, to life and purse
Sworn foes,—Cock-Horse, Hobgoblin, Ghost,
Chimæra, Atomy, or worse
Than ever brain of childhood crossed,
  Or lived in legend of a nurse?
Say, can we hope to keep the peace
Without patrols and male police?"

XXXVIII.

Thus she. Sibylla answered straight,
(Inspired priestess, who receives
From Progress all designs of Fate,
And oracles in mystery weaves.*
Nor loves she to vaticinate,
Like Cumæ's seer, from scattered leaves, †
But in her cave mankind invites
To patch up Truth from " Broken Lights ") :

XXXIX.

" Too well, though dark, your words confess
Your heathen God, unhappy maid ;
How many a fair idolatress
In the old world has he betrayed,

---

* Here is a specimen of a modern oracle, which, for caution and ambiguity, may stand comparison with anything that ever came out of Delphi :—

"Such, we may hope, may be the progress of human thought, and the process of the growth of the religion of the Future, if it be allowed to expand naturally and beautifully. If, on the other hand, the opposition against it be so bitter, and the forces of Traditionalism ranged so determinately in opposition as to bar every step of advance, then, indeed, none may say what course things may take. Reformation arrested becomes Revolution. On him who would stop the wheels of the Chariot of Progress must lie the blame of the inevitable overthrow that will ensue."—*Broken Lights*, by FRANCES POWER COBBE. It must be acknowledged that this feminine way of "hedging" a prophecy is uncommonly neat.

† " Verum eadem, verso tenuis quum cardine ventus
    Impulit, et teneras turbavit janua frondes,
    Nunquam deinde cavo volitantia prendere saxo,
    Nec revocare situs, aut jungere carmina curat :
    Inconsulti abeunt, sedemque odere Sibyllæ."—VIRG.: *Æn.* 3, 448.

Love, once adjudged divine! nor less
His idle spectre has been laid
With Bourbons, crinolines, and crochet,
Ever since the days of Abbé Fauchet.*

XL.

"The little fool is never found
Where Women have abjured the needle;
In all our clubs he is discrowned;
And now the veriest Parish Beadle
May clap him in the Stocks or Pound,
Like Hudibras, howe'er he wheedle;
So banished hence, a pretty tune
He's like to whistle in the Moon.

XLI.

"On earth I own no science shows
How singly to prolong existence;
The Moon fresh methods may disclose.
As for those beasts that at this distance
You fear,—all colonists have foes.
Have we not Truth, Tracts, Steam, Rods, Pistons?
Doubt you with these our mighty era
May civilize the worst chimæra?

---

* The masculine exponent of "Woman's Rights" in the French Revolution.

XLII.

"Me, me my God, swift Progress, showed
   The Moon's far future in my cell:
There saw I telegraph and road,
   Old Tycho spanned by female Fell;
Beside the Sea of Clouds abode
   Our judges; by the Pit of Hell*
I saw (O joyful Revolution!)
A Working Woman's Institution.

XLIII.

"Then fear not from Mankind to elope,
   Fair Celia, nor to Love hold fast,
But seek this College of Good Hope,
   Hired by our wise Iconoclast.
And now let all who with clear scope
   The Future seize, who hate the Past,
To Progress bend the reverent knee,
And make high sacrifice with me!"

XLIV.

She said: and, with her hair undone,
   Of twelve band-boxes made a pyre;
Bright balls of worsted, half a ton,
   Succeed; love-letters pile it higher:

---

* This is only a mountain, dear reader, in the N. hemisphere of the Moon.

And next, of nine fair pug-dogs one
She chose by lot to feed the fire : *
Thy thread, poor Beau, the eternal Shears
Then cut, nor pitied Celia's tears.

XLV.

The torch is lit ; up shoot the flames ;
Sibylla for the maddening crews
A solemn Commination frames :
" Cursèd be she who deigns to use
The needle, who no Franchise claims ;
Who has no faith in Broad Church 'views,' †
Or of our holy priests makes japes ;
Who think all women once were apes.

---

* A customary rite in all ages at high sacrifices. Achilles made the same offering to the shade of Patroclus :

"'Εννεα τῷ γε ἄνακτι τραπεζῆες κύνες ἦσαν,
Καὶ μὲν τῶν ἐνέβαλλε πυρῃ δύο δειροτομήσας."

" Of nine large dogs, domestic at his board,
Fall two, selected to attend their lord."—POPE.

† The Rev. Fred. W. Higginson, U. S., evidently has but a small acquaintance with England. He says, " Every woman in Massachusetts has her 'views' upon every subject. It is true that English women have superb frames, grand muscles, fine energies, that they speak two or three languages, but then they usually don't have any 'views :' and, thank God, I live in a State where women have them."—*Report of Seventh Women's-Rights Convention*, p. 33.

XLVI.

'Cursèd be she by all the Nine,
  Who swears an oath by Venus' doves;
  Who sends or gets a Valentine;
  Who wins at Ascot bet of gloves;
  Who pays no vows at Progress' shrine,
  Or votive thimble hangs in Love's:
  Cursèd be she who looks on men."
And all but Celia said "Amen!"

XLVII.

But she, though feigning to submit,
  Recalls, poor maid, her luckless Beau:
  How on hind legs he used to sit
  With pendent paws of speechless woe;
  His courtly parts, his native wit,
  His tail,—and now a shade below!
  The locket heaving on her breast,
  And trembling lip, her grief confessed.

XLVIII.

Meantime Cornelia's winged Thought
  Soared from the cavern of her brain,
  And the vast void of vacuum sought:
  Through two score miles of wind and rain
  It passed; then to the limits brought
  The nymphs of Light relieved its pain,
  Bore it through easy space, and soon
  Set down the traveller in the Moon.

XLIX.

Now in the Moon the outcast Gods
Abode; for since mankind's ingratitude
Had ploughed Olympus into clods,
And Ordnance surveys found Heaven's latitude,
Jove, seeing all his awful nods
Unheeded, and himself a platitude,
Resolved to leave this world and us,
Leading a heavenly Exodus.

L.

So after endless voyages,
Hovering in space, like flocks of Gannet,
And sick for their primeval ease,
At last they pitched upon this planet;
And charmed with what are called its "seas," *
(Just as we say the "Isle of Thanet")
Made a mock heaven—as Madam Hector
A Troy—beside the Sea of Nectar.

LI.

But stranger and more awful far
Is that new heaven; for there no hum
Of life is heard; no trade nor war
Disturb the silence; all is dumb.

---

* "Of old the name of 'Seas' was given to the large dark spots which mottle the Moon's northern hemisphere and part of the southern one towards the west and east. The name is still retained, though its literal meaning must not be attached to it. The lunar seas are now regarded as plains."—*The Heavens*, p. 141.

Over the vast and voiceless star
No momentary motions come.
No wind, nor fire, nor snow, nor rain,
Shall ever beat its face again.

LII.

Or if at times some loosened rock
Dash down the mountain, bound on bound,
Crag meeting crag in thunder shock
Of conflict, yet there comes no sound.
Such battle seems the more to mock
The melancholy peace around;
As he who living passed in dread
The voiceless gapings of the Dead.*

LIII.

Oft the deep silences arouse
Thoughts of some ancient human reign;
And if 'twas ever populous
With mortal pleasure, love, and pain;
So in some old and empty house
We feel the fever of our brain,
That warmth, and breath, and speech revives,
And footfalls of a thousand lives.

---

* "At Danaûm proceres Agamemnoniæque phalanges,
　　Ut videre virum, fulgentiaque arma per umbras,
　　Ingenti trepidare metu: pars vertere terga,
　　Ceu quondam petiere rates; pars tollere vocem
　　Exiguam: inceptus clamor frustratur hiantes."
　　　　　　　　　　　　VIRG.: *Æn.* 6, 490.

LIV.

Strange Humour all the place attires;
Sweet Paradox the fancy wakes;
There with the Sun the starry choirs
Shine unabashed, like morning rakes;
There the volcanoes have no fires;
There is no water in the lakes;
The axis through the airless deep
Whirls on, but moves not, in its sleep.

LV.

Hence it may be that here post-haste,
By some magnetical attraction,
Flies up (for Nature knows no waste)
Man's every foolish thought and action.
This astronomic truth you traced,
And proved the same to satisfaction,
Who first the Moon's far frontiers crossed, O
Poet of Poets, Ariosto.*

---

* See the exquisitely ironical Canto xxxiv. of the *Orlando Furioso*. St. John mounts with Astulph into the Moon, the store-house of all human vanities. In Ariosto's poem everything is represented as dead. I give one stanza as a sample of his description:—

> " Le lacrime e i sospiri degli amanti,
> L'inutil tempo che si perde a giuoco,
> E l'ozio lungo d'uomini ignoranti,
> Vani disegni che non han mai loco;
> I vani disideri sono tanti
> Che la più parte ingombran di quel loco:
> Ciò che in somma quaggiù perdesti mai,
> Lassù salendo ritrovar potai."

The advance of astronomy since the days of Ariosto alone encourages me to transform the conception of the most inimitable of poets.

LVI.

For Thought, that is of Silence born,
Return to its own country craves,
And from man's brain set free, forlorn,
Flies wandering over hills and waves;
Yet neither in the quiet corn
Finds refuge, no, nor in the graves.
The air with life seems all atune;
At last it seeks the airless Moon.

LVII.

Behind each Thought the wingèd Words
Mount in the livery of their Master:
Much swifter they than swiftest birds,
But Thought than lightning-flash is faster;
So when they pass the air that girds
Our planet, these endure disaster,
And Space being lighter far than Sound,
They sink to the infinite profound.

LVIII.

But the swift Thoughts, like Mercury shod,
Now mounted to their goal, assume
Their thinker's form, and to each God
Make play, like spectres of the tomb:
Pleased with a spectacle so odd,
The Gods, who first were plunged in gloom,
Made them a stage, and ever after
Called it the Paradise of Laughter.

LIX.

And here they sit, and age by age
Still finds them in the same pursuit,
The ceaseless silent pilgrimage
Of actors, and the audience mute,
A man might deem it was the stage
Of Athens, wanting voice and flute,
The drama his, save for the words,
Who made the Cloud-Town of the Birds.

LX.

Ah! could we to that Play-house pass,
And learn what all this mystery means,
How should we then our world re-class!
There naked thought no language screens,
Each is as true as to his glass,
And plays his life behind the scenes.
The Gods with silent joy surprise
Bright laughter in each other's eyes.

LXI.

From North, and South, and East, and West,
They see uprising into light
The buried silence of each breast,
Dark Thoughts of Vanity and Night;
Ambitions, Envies unexpressed,
Dim Fears that language hid from sight,
And all the heart most deeply feels,
And hence most virtuously conceals.

LXII.

Here meet all ages, bond and free,
Greeks, Turks, Gauls, Germans, Jews, Circassians,
All that is thought on land or sea,
King's secrets, and the ploughman's passions,
Unsurpliced priest, or devotee
Pondering in church on Paris fashions,
Or poet in a Hymn to Duty
Startled by sudden "Et tu, Brute!"

LXIII.

Ye Gods, whom Thought alone can reach,
Consider ye our world is spinning
With roar and rise of Babel speech,
Just as it was in the beginning;
Yet each with heart unknown to each,
Goes ever struggling, losing, winning,
And of his neighbour talks so loud
That self is silenced in the crowd?

LXIV.

Now as like gentles of Vandyke
The Gods reposed, it chanced (for lately,
From New York West to Eastern Sikh,
Thoughts had come sadly and sedately,
All as respectably alike
As syllogisms of Mill or Whately)
Phœbus, the actors to inspire,
Rang out this ballad on his lyre:

LXV.

" Laughter, last legacy of Earth
   Left to the Gods, light child of Folly,
   For loved by Wit she gave thee birth,
   Sister to Love and Melancholy ;
   Thou art the maiden friend of Mirth,
   Nor yet to tears a stranger wholly ;
   Sweeter than nectar that they quaff
   To hearts celestial is to laugh.

LXVI.

" Though on a world grown inly cold,
   For evermore we ride through Space,
   Though roofless lie in Pæstum old
   The ruined temples of our race :
   Which, dreaming still an Age of Gold,
   With Age of Dollars men replace ;
   If geese be swans, and wheat seem chaff,
   More reason for the Gods to laugh.

LXVII.

" The Earth of old was made with rings,
   That fell like fire-flakes from the Sun ;
   Hence sprang the Apes, to Apes the Kings
   Succeeded, now their sand is run ;
   The needy bard the People sings,
   The Many press upon the One ;
   Yet after all, 'tis half and half,
   The Many talk, the One may laugh.

LXVIII.

"For men must pass; the Many miss
True Wisdom; mortal is each state;
Only the Soul immortal is,
Disdain and Envy, Love and Hate,
And thou, O Laughter, even in this
More strong than Kings, since free from Fate;
Let Clotho hold the threads and staff;
Come weal, come woe, the Gods shall laugh."

LXIX.

He ceased: nor had a mortal ear
Known he had sung: no echoes roll,
As through our airs terrestrial here;
But Silence sounds from soul to soul.
And now Cornelia's Thought grew clear
Before them: o'er their hearts then stole
Fresh Laughter, for in form and feature
They ne'er had seen so strange a creature.

LXX.

Her wig with travel was awry,
From top to toe she looked one blue;
Yet told her tale with gestures high,
And faced unawed the heavenly crew.
These first looked on with laughing eye,
Soon in their hearts strange horror grew;
Cold the celestial ichor ran;
Silent they sat, till Jove began:

LXXI.

" Are we those deities who rolled
　　Destruction on the impious giants?
And sit we timorous now and cold,
　　Shrinking at Woman's weak defiance?
Alas! we are not the gods of old;
　　Our bolts will barely match man's science:
Bolts did I say? In this cold world
There's not a fireball to be hurled.

LXXII.

" But while we lack even arms like these,
　　Behold on earth what things are done;
They've bored the mountains, bridged the seas,
　　Their wires beneath the ocean run;
To utmost air they mount with ease;
　　'Tis said they've even weighed the sun;*
Typhoeus' old unwieldy plot
Had thriven, had he been leagued with Watt.

LXXIII.

" Some think these women's hearts to gain.
　　Fools! will they yield to our embrace,
Like Danae or Alcmena fain?
　　Stars then we gave them for their grace;

---

* " The weight of the Sun may thus be expressed in tons :—
　　2,154,106,580,000,000,000,000,000,000.
It ranks, as we see, among those numbers which present nothing to the mind, and leave the imagination itself powerless."—*The Heavens*, p. 25.

The Stars themselves they now attain;
Besides I own—Cornelia's face!
O friends! what boots it to be brave,
If neither Love nor War can save?

LXXIV.

"Home of the Gods! was ever Lar
So travel-tost by Time as yours?
What world so perilous or far,
But Man some entrance there procures?
Oh where's the planet or fixed star
Safe from Commissioners of Sewers?
But those who counsel war or flight,
Now speak. Arede, ye Gods, aright."

LXXV.

Then answered Love—for Love the most
At bold Cornelia's message smarts,
For all the Gods had heard him boast,
Lord, so he said, of women's hearts—
"Have you, my sire, indeed so lost
All memory of those mortal parts?
Well! If Jove's love to moonshine fades
Let our Diana speak for maids.*

---

* Diana, it is scarcely necessary to inform my readers, had a secret love affair with Endymion.

LXXVI.

"Too long, since we left home in Greece,
  You've let the world grow fat in order;
Love only dares disturb Man's peace,
  And still contests the airy Border.
Little care I for his police;
I laugh to scorn each grim Recorder:
Still I go free the whole earth through,
Still all Lucretius said is true.

LXXVII.

"But knowing all the mortal world,
  I've fathomed most the female sex,
And woman's banner, when unfurled,
  Bears still this motto,—'I perplex.'
Laugh on, though all her threats be hurled,
Nor let this Thought your courage vex.
The cause be mine; the boastful foe
Shall find that Love has still a bow."

LXXVIII.

So spoke the Babe, and seemed to swell
  With pride; already he's afield;
His stature rises to an ell;
  Proudly he calls for shaft and shield:
Nor did he read the future well,
Nor Atropos his fate revealed;
For well alone of all their kind
Are Love and Justice painted blind.

LXXIX.

Then round him pressed each Heavenly Dame;
Some pat his shoulder, pinch his cheek,
Some from his lips sweet kisses claim,
And curtsey with mock reverence meek.
Only Diana, for pure shame,
Was silent, shot with arrowy pique;
For, keeping still her virgin tone
Austere, she'd hoped her loves unknown.

LXXX.

Now of his little wingèd grooms
One his light bow and quiver gets,
Another smooths his shining plumes,
A third his shafts on moonstone whets;
This gives his golden curls new blooms,
And brings him charms and amulets,
Armlets, and rings in nightly raid
Oft stol'n from fair unrobing maid.

LXXXI.

They arm his brow, and set thereon
A star, like glowworm's lamp when eves
Grow warmer; on his bosom shone
The Garter, hope of amorous thieves;
And, more to enchant each female don,
He wore blue stockings for his greaves;
Hoping they'd take himself to be
A Doctor of Divinity.

LXXXII.

Besides, to increase the pleasing dream,
A cap and gown Minerva brought,
Last memories of her Academe;
Then Mercury's sandals he besought.
Such arms unvanquishable seem,
Matched with Cornelia's maiden Thought;
And sweetly laughed the Gods above,
Saying, " How high a lord is Love!"

BOOK II.

ARGUMENT.

LOVE, having descended to Cornelia's College, falls asleep in the garden, where, being found by Celia, and awaked, he shoots his arrows at the Women, and is whipped by Sibylla and Cornelia. Returning to the Moon, he is mocked by Hercules, but shows the Gods Cornelia's glove, the vast size of which inspires them with terror. Upon this Saturn upbraids Jove for his desire of change, and shows the result of Whiggism; and Jove in turn casting the blame upon Minerva and her Philosophers, they are both rebuked by Venus, who bids them leave all consideration of what is changeable in Man, and to reflect instead on the eternal and immutable conditions of human passion. She declares her intention of taking the field, and then flies to the Cave of Momus, gaoler of Men's Dreams and Vanities, from whom she begs assistance. Being furnished by Momus with an idle Dream, she sends him to the Earth, and he, visiting the soul of Amadis in his sleep, persuades him that a new era of chivalry has begun, and inspires him, in emulation of Britomart, to enter Cornelia's College in woman's attire. Amadis, setting forth upon his adventure, finds the Women sitting round a fountain in their quadrangle, and is matriculated into the College.

BOOK II.

I.

DAN PHŒBUS, with the Crab, once more
Had waked the earth to hear the ditty
That the first nightingales out-pour,
And frogs in amorous committee,
When Love, the little Bachelor,
To war with maidens old or pretty,
Left the Moon's circle, and came down
To mortals, clad in cap and gown.

II.

Our earth he reached, with many a sneeze
Descending; round his every limb
The air grew purple, and the seas;
Bright larks in troop escorted him,
And swandown, buoyant on the breeze.
So fared he, and when day was dim,
Tired with his travel since the dawn,
Dropt on Cornelia's College lawn.

III.

Here o'er the grass the immortal Boy
Went dancing through the dews and flowers:
It makes his bosom move with joy
To feel the young light-hearted Hours,
That by green bush and bankside toy
On Earth's deep bosom fresh with showers,
The leaves new-born, and everything
Wistful awhile in Hope and Spring.

IV.

Soon, while the darkening leaves are stirred
By sleepy linnets in the willows,
And scarce a human sound is heard,
His head upon his arm he pillows,
And soothed by one melodious bird,
Forgetting all his peccadilloes,
And all his arts and counsels deep,
And bow and arrows,—falls asleep.

V.

Now, while he slept, unto that part
Cornelia came; for the sweet time
Had moved strange pleasure in her heart:
Came Pastorella, skilled in rhyme;
Sibylla, Grotia, one in art,
And one in prophecy sublime;
And Lydia frank, and more as well,
All known to fame, "but long to tell."

VI.

Cornelia, who the day had spent
Modelling Republics, Greek or Roman,
Now, in sweet relaxation, bent
Her wise discourse upon a gnomon.
All up and down the grass-plot went,
Regardless of the little bowman,
Who, 'neath a rosebush, just aside,
Lay unespying, unespied.

VII.

But Celia, all alone and free,
Behind this company-had strayed in
A labyrinth of sweet reverie
Because her soul was heavy laden
With knowledge. On a sudden she
Came on the sleeping God. The maiden
Sprang back, and felt her bosom's kernel
Pierced through with soft desires maternal.

VIII.

One arm out of his sleeve was cast,
And his loose quiver's scarlet thread
Across his snowy bosom passed;
His cap lay by his curly head.
Celia stooped down and caught him fast,
Then with a thousand kisses, sped
Among her sisterhood to bring
Sight of this new and strange plaything.

IX.

Love, thus aroused, winked, stared, then laughed,
And, still in Celia's bosom, drew
His silken string, while shaft on shaft
He shot like sunbeams ; but the crew,
Who now too late perceived his craft,
Fled past as Dryads o'er the dew ;
Mixed pleasure, pain, and fear they feel,
And wounds they scarcely care to heal.

X.

While Celia stanched her bosom's flow,
Yet held the archer on his perch,
Cornelia snatched the Babe, and now
The bold Sibylla flies to search
For weapon from the penal bough.
'Tis found : Cornelia takes the birch :
The tyrant, like a netted fly,
Kicks idly, then begins to cry.

XI.

But all in vain ; the rod bestains
His back with red, and, " Let your play be
Confined," she cries, "to idle brains,
And hearts of men ! Go, foolish Baby,
And tell your mother of your pains ;
Bear, too, Cornelia's glove : it may be
She, if she seek these haunts, even she,
Shall fare the same :" then sets him free.

XII.

Back, like a wounded duck, he flew,
With crippled wings and broken bow ;
The Stars wept down redoubled dew,
And pitying bats bewailed his woe ;
But Wisdom's bird, with loud "Tu-whoo!"
Spied from the barn his ancient foe,
And left his mice, and through the night
Pressed hooting on the Archer's flight.

XIII.

Scarce had he crossed the immediate miles
Of Space, when oh !- what tongue can say
How Heaven broke out in radiant smiles?
Was this, they thought, the Champion gay
Who, in his beauty and his wiles,
Went out to war at break of day?
But while the more part speechless sit,
Alcides thus approves his wit:

XIV.

" Hail Conqueror! Yet, methinks, the fight
Has cost our Cupid dear in plumes :
What brooch-pin, what stiletto bright
Robbed you in battle of your blooms?
Describe what arrowy needle flight
You felt, what bottles of perfumes.
Did Nemean Kitten, hard to die,
Wound you, or Cerberus fetched from Skye?" *

---

* Alcides takes occasion to reflect with more point on the weakness

XV.

But as some Pygmy, whose escape
Is noised abroad, in Falstaff's vein
Paints to the crowd the enormous shape,
Legs, bill, and pinions of the Crane;
So Cupid tells them of his rape,
His idle arrows, and his pain;
"Giants," he cries, "have vanquished Love,"—
Then shows for proof Cornelia's glove.

XVI.

Around the glove the Immortals come,
And view the vast expanse of thread,
How huge a gulf betwixt the thumb
And the forefinger there is spread.
The five tall steeples strike them dumb,
The five dark caverns : all is dread;
Silent and sad upon such foes
They pondered; then old Saturn rose.

XVII.

"O slow to reason and foresee!
Think you, son Jove, these things are strange?
Men deal by you as you by me;
Know this is all the work of Change.

---

of Love by alluding to what Strength had accomplished in the Labours of the Nemean Lion and the removal of Cerberus from Hell.

Fool! who perceived not what must be
When once you'd let the Giants range,
And doomed those old protected crops
That peaceful Saturn tilled with Ops!*

XVIII.

" Once with fair elbow-room on earth
I ruled a loyal race, though rude ;
Produce sufficient, and no dearth :
No city paupers cried for food.
And if my children at the birth
I swallowed, the intent was good ;
Nature's inevitable law
Before wise Malthus I foresaw.

XIX.

" But you, forsooth, had clearer lights ;
You said your Principles were higher,
And feigning zeal for abstract Rights,
Drove from his throne your poor old sire.

---

* Combining the Greek and Roman myths, the story of Saturn may be told thus :—He was an old God-King who presided over a golden feudal age of Aristocracy and Protection in the company of Ops, his wife. He, however (as the followers of M. Comte advise in our own day), practised infanticide, and his son Jove was only saved from this fate by the substitution of a stone. Jove, making his father's malpractices a plea for revolt, turned him out of his kingdom, and inaugurated the modern constitutional era. He held his throne with persistent but precarious tenure, owing to the risings of the Giants, till his final expulsion from Olympus.

Soon (so the changer Change requites)
Prometheus rose, and stealing fire,
For all your wise Caucasian plan,
Outwitted you, instructing Man.

XX.

" Then on the earth mankind increased :
Yet, boasting none could cut their comb,
Race swallowed Race ; the conquered East
Was food for Greece, and Greece for Rome ;
In Rome arose a new High-priest,
And crowned a Goth in Cæsar's home ;
The Goth's turn came ; his Slaves rebelled,
And, copying you, their Kings expelled.

XXI.

" The first were English Charles and James ;
Next from the scene poor Louis passed ;
To-day have gone two Bourbon names,
Bomba, and Isabel the last ;
Now kingless Man all nature claims,
Yet vainly hopes his anchor cast,
His Monarchs ousted, now the ban
He feels ; the Woman ousts the Man.

XXII.

" The Women, still for change athirst,
Fly from their crowded globe, and soon
The Maids, whom you pursued at first
On earth, will drive you from the Moon.

Thus in full circle are you cursed.
Now must you live, a lazy loon,
On parish rates, or beg, or dig.
Lo! this it is to be a Whig!"

XXIII.

"Nay," Jove replied, with moody brows,
"Fate, and not blindness, was my bane;
For, leagued with me against your House,
The Giants but secured my reign.
And why did I the Estates espouse?
To hang all Heaven from my gold chain; *
Freedom was never my intent;
' Le ciel c'est moi!' was all I meant.

---

* Iliad, viii. 18 :—

"Εἰ δ' ἄγε πειρήσασθε, θέοι, ἵνα εἴδετε πάντες,
σειρὴν χρυσείην ἐξ οὐρανόθεν κρεμάσαντες,
πάντες δ' ἐξάπτεσθε θεοί πᾶσαί τε θέαιναι·
Ἀλλ' οὐκ ἂν ἐρύσαιτ' ἐξ οὐρανόθεν πεδίονδε
Ζῆν' ὕπατον μήστωρ', οὐδ' εἰ μάλα πολλὰ κάμοιτε·
Ἀλλ' ὅτε δὴ καὶ ἐγὼ πρόφρων ἐθέλοιμι ἐρύσσαι,
Αὐτῇ κεν γαίῃ ἐρύσαιμ' αὐτῇ τε θαλάσσῃ·
σειρὴν μέν κεν ἔπειτα περὶ ῥίον Οὐλύμποιο
Δησαίμην, τὰ δέ κ'αὐτα μετήορα πάντα γένοιτο·
Τόσσον ἐγὼ περὶ τ'εἰμὶ θεῶν περὶ τ'εἰμ' ἀνθρώπων."

"League all your forces then, ye powers above,
Join all, and try the Omnipotence of Jove:
Let down our golden everlasting chain,
Whose strong embrace holds heaven, and earth, and main;
Strive all, of mortal and immortal birth,
To drag by this the Thunderer down to earth. ["Ye

XXIV.

"Then Tax, Indemnity, and Trade,
  Rank, Office, all things leaned on me;
Pluto was Justice of the Shade
  By purchase, Neptune of the Sea;
The Giants my each nod obeyed;
  They never dreamed they were not free.
Then who, oh, who, my dream cut short?
My child, the darling of my Court!

XXV.

"Minerva, whose old harmless walk
  Was with her spiders in the air,
Chose all my policy to balk,
  And spoke your fallen Titans fair,*
Teaching each earth-born ass to talk,
  And every fool to play Voltaire.
Father, my fate should be my plea;
I cheated you, my daughter me."

"Ye strive in vain! If I but stretch this hand,
  I heave the Gods, the ocean, and the land:
I fix the chain to great Olympus' height,
  And the vast world hangs trembling in my sight!
For such I reign unbounded and above,
  And such are men and Gods compared to Jove."—POPE.

* Minerva, in some myths, is represented as playing the same part to Jove as the Philosophers to the French Kings, and helping Prometheus to steal the fire from Heaven.

XXVI.

Up sprang the gold-haired Cyprian Queen:
" O Heavens! and have the Gods turned gapers,
Listening in awe while these declaim
Like journalists in morning papers?
Such penny politics may frame
A nine-days' wonder for the drapers;
But have the Gods no subtler arts
To use, the Gods who read men's hearts?

XXVII.

" How vain to dwell on Man's new powers,
If Man's old impotence we leave,
Knowing the Thoughts of all the hours
Since here we came on Christmas Eve!
Say, where's the passion Change devours?
Do men still Hope, Hate, Envy, Grieve?
Science, supreme o'er mortals' gloves,
Dwarfs not, nor can dilate their Loves.

XXVIII.

" No! changed in manners, language, dress,
They come the same from age to age,
Like pieces on a board at Chess,
To solve their problems on our stage.
Vast seem their arts and limitless
When in free conflict they engage;
Yet kept by fate in certain grooves,
What if the Gods direct the moves?

XXIX.

" Love in his person took the field,
    Daring the maids to open fight,
So Love himself was forced to yield,
    As boys at Chess who play not right;
Myself will play, but unrevealed,
    Matching the Black against the White.
If men meet maids, whate'er's between,
My Knight may take Cornelia's Queen.

XXX.

" For where proud mortals boast so loud
    The Gods should play a silent game.
Virtue's chief castle is the Crowd;
    For there, from self-deceit or shame,
Each seeks his inward doubts to shroud,
    While all the general faith proclaim;
Surprise the braggarts, each and each,
Presto! their valour ends in speech.

XXXI.

" I go, this College with dark arts
    To mine, not battering at the gate,
But while they suffer from Love's darts,
    My troops in secret, early, late,
Shall close each passage round their hearts,
    Till in good time I cry 'Check-mate!'
Then, scourged with their own impious rods,
Maids shall submit, and fear the Gods."

XXXII.

She said, resolved on counsels wise,
And her deep heart divined a spell;
Then with her deathless doves she flies
To the Moon's mountain named of Hell,
Where all men's Thoughts and Vanities
In deep sublunar prison dwell,
Many a dark Dream, and many a wing
Fast bound, and Momus is their King.

XXXIII.

There is a dark and silent den,
Driven 'neath the mountain's basement far;
Huge rocks of cheerless shade impen
The place with vast volcanic bar.
Hence fly they forth, here mount again,
Man's torments, brood of angry star;
Each Thought returning brings release
To one in prison : there is no cease.

XXXIV.

Within, around the rifted roof,
Dim Fears and Follies bat-like flit;
Here brood dark Cares, and there aloof
Megrims and Melancholies sit;
Here sages Systems, far from Proof,
Spin finest webs; distempered Wit
Watches o'er Hopes, that still mistime
The statesman's thought, or rave in rhyme.

XXXV.

Dim Shadows crowd the gloomy aisles,
Clinging to wall, and roof, and floor;
Dreams over Dreams, close huddling files,
Waning into the darkness, more
Than birds that blacken the Orkney isles,
Or coast by northern Labrador.
So wait they, and when Fate has spun
The appointed thread, each sees the sun.

XXXVI.

Day after day, like Plato's souls,*
The circling incorporeal swarms
Move round between our earthly poles,
And each some mortal brain informs;
When the grim gaoler backward rolls
The gate, then, like the Æolian storms,
Those freed by Fate whirl forth apace,
These fresh from travel fill their place.

XXXVII.

But when new Thoughts arrive on earth,
First, all the ambient airs they trouble,
Whose motion makes men's brains give birth.
Then Companies blow many a bubble;

---

* For the account of the circular motion of Souls, see Plato, *Timæus*, 41, D. E.

Each Journal finds the cynic's mirth
Fresh food ; Philosophers see double ;
All sporting Augurs spawn dark hints ;
And every Bard his spasms prints.

XXXVIII.

Before the cavern with his keys
Sits Momus, gaoler grim but wise,
His head up-pillared from his knees
On his two palms ; his inward eyes
Move not (and hence the world he sees) : *
Or if new captives bid him rise,
Still dreaming, he unbars the door,
Shuts it, then falls in thought once more.

---

* "Ὁ γοῦν Μῶμος ἀκήκοας οἶμαι ἅτινα ᾐτιάσατο τοῦ Ἡφαίστου, εἰ δὲ μή, ἀλλὰ νῦν ἄκουε. φησὶ γὰρ ὁ μῦθος ἐρίσαι Ἀθηνᾶν καὶ Ποσειδῶνα καὶ Ἥφαιστον εὐτεχνίας πέρι, καὶ τὸν μὲν Ποσειδῶ ταῦρόν τινα ἀναπλάσαι, τὴν Ἀθηνᾶν δὲ οἰκίαν ἐπινοῆσαι. ὁ Ἥφαιστος δὲ ἄνθρωπον ἄρα συνεστήσατο. καὶ ἐπείπερ ἐπὶ τὸν Μῶμον ἧκον, ὅνπερ δικάστην προείλοντο, θεασάμενος ἐκεῖνος ἑκάστου τὸ ἔργον, τῶν μὲν ἄλλων ἅτινα ᾐτιάσατο περιττὸν ἂν εἴη λέγειν· ἐπὶ τοῦ ἀνθρώπου δὲ τοῦτο ἐμέμψατο, καὶ τὸν ἀρχιτέκτονα ἐπέπληξε τὸν Ἥφαιστον, διότι μὴ καὶ θυρίδας ἐποίησεν αὐτῷ κατὰ τὸ στέρνον, ὡς ἀναπετασθεισῶν γνώριμα γενέσθαι ἅπασιν ἃ βούλεται καὶ ἐπινοεῖ, καὶ εἰ ψεύδεται ἢ ἀληθεύει."

"At any rate you have heard, I suppose, of the fault that Momus found with Vulcan ; but if you have not, hear now. The myth says that Minerva, Neptune, and Vulcan disputed which was the best artist, and that Neptune made a bull, and Minerva invented a house. Vulcan, however, composed a man. And when they were come to Momus, whom they had chosen judge, he examined the work of each, and found certain blemishes in the two first of which we need not speak ; but the fault which he found in man, and for which he blamed Vulcan who made him, was this, that he had not made him doors also in his breast, which might be opened for all to know his wishes and thoughts, and whether he speaks false or true."—LUCIAN : *Hermotimus.*

XXXIX.

Thus his own bosom's watchful spy,
He finds why Love is born of leisure;
Why youth and maid by change of eye
Thrill to the heart, and whence their pleasure;
Men's souls he fathoms, men who die,
Yet shrink to bound by mortal measure
Desires of Glory, Power, or Pelf,
All this he finds within himself.

XL.

To him the Goddess came and said,
" Momus, when all the Immortals fear,
Sitt'st thou thus still with dreaming head?
Surely to see thee is good cheer,
For of the living and the dead
Thou knowest, all hearts to thee are clear;
But rise, thou silent sage, and soon,
Or we and thou must lose the Moon.

XLI.

" For never yet our earth-born foe,
Proud Science, reared her head so high,
Lifting the hearts of maids below
To invade the empire of the sky.
But these thou knewest long ago,
Hast seen them born, and breathe, and die;
Join now thyself to Venus' arts,
And let thy Dreams assail their hearts.

XLII.

" Were mortals all upon one side,
The Gods might wage a desperate strife;
But rivalries their host divide;
'Twixt man and maid disputes are rife;
Then let us, with mankind allied,
Inspire some youth to steal a wife
From proud Cornelia's maids, who seek
To fly to Heaven, and prove them weak."

XLIII.

Then smiling rose that gaoler sage,
And backward rolled the ponderous gate,
Beckoning from out his darksome cage
A Dream, lean, withered, out of date.
Full many an old romantic page
He'd madden'd, many a poet's pate,
In every age vain wishes cast,
Shadowing the Future and the Past.

XLIV.

Once had he lodged in Cato's heart,
And after in Don Quixote's brain;
Then painted, by Lamartine's art,
The new Republic's golden reign.
Thrown on each trial, with fresh start
The brain-born giant rose again.
Him to the Queen the gaoler led,
Then sat, and once more bowed his head.

XLV.

But Love's bright Queen the Dream addressed,—
" Dream! from all mortal sight and sound
Secure! dark secret of unrest!
Hence to thy goal, wherever bound!
But oh! if ever in man's breast
Thou didst stir Fancy, or confound
Reason, or move to Love's delight,
Now be four times thyself to-night.

XLVI.

" And for thy weapons, take with thee
These arrows, forged of bright moonbeam,
Wherewith by the Sicilian Sea
I shot the heart of Polypheme.*
Thou, with thine arts in thy degree,
Canst cause a young man's brain to dream,
And these, with poisons from above,
Shall fire his wounded soul to love."

---

* " ἔχθιστον ἔχων ὑποκάρδιον ἕλκος,
Κύπριδος ἐκ μεγάλας τό οἱ ἥπατι πᾶξε βέλεμνον."

" With the death-wound in his breast, which the arrow of great Venus fixed in his heart."—THEOCRITUS, Id. xi. 16.

XLVII.

She said : the Dream in haste to obey,
Shot earthwards from the lunar steep :
Soon came he where a city lay,
Lamplit, and silent, and asleep :
He passes many a darkened way,
And many a door of slumber deep,
Bat-like to eaves and casement clings,
And fans the roofs with noiseless wings.

XLVIII.

Here dwelt one Amadis, whose star
(If by improvidence of date,
Or envious hope his life to mar)
Had borne him centuries too late.
No man so many thoughts afar
Had sent into the lunar state,
For there was none alive whose birth
Had fallen so far behind the earth.

XLIX.

His birth was due when orient beams
Of Hope and Fancy waked each breast ;
When half the world was in men's dreams,
And piled with jewels, east and west ;
When first, as over Lethe streams,
The Admirals through Atlantic pressed,
And brought you from the jaws of Death
Glory and gold, Elizabeth.

L.

When, in despite of Virtue's frown,
Great sinners still out-topped the age;
When from high heaven the Gods came down,
And buskined trod the sceneless stage;
When wit and odours shared the Town,
(Yet wit prevailed o'er sewerage),
When Shakespeare broke (ye Poets, shame!)
The laws of Duty and of Game.

LI.

But his Soul slept, and now when Time,
Who even as men makes nations hoary,
Touching his country's noble prime,
Had left the Gold but stolen the Glory,
When there was nothing left for rhyme,
And Knighthood was an empty story,
He woke, and by his Star was made
A poet in a time of trade.

LII.

As once the Ephesian, waking late,
Went forth, unwitting of the year,
And saw the Cross above the Gate—
The Cross adored in secret fear
But yesterday;—soon many a mate
He missed, and many a comrade dear;
Yet knew not his own hair was white,
Dreaming he had but slept a night:

LIII.

So was this Amadis forlorn:
His brain was full of Knights and lances,
And deeds achieved ere he was born;
Books were his world; his men were fancies;
Still in his dreams rang Roland's horn
So clear, that all his circumstances
Seemed but a Masque, the passing Age
The Players, and his own heart the Stage.

LIV.

Had he in old La Mancha lived,
Sancho had cleaned a second spear;
But now the nations had survived
Don Quixote many and many a year,
And though men still ate, drank, and wived,
Yet, buying cheap and selling dear,
There'd scarce been found at his last breath
A barber to bewail his death.

LV.

Now, as became a valorous Knight,
This youth meet homage paid to Beauty,
But being in truth an ill-starred wight,
'Twas Celia claimed his love and duty—
Celia, whom ravished from his sight
A modern Giant kept as booty,
Strong as that Mage who did bewitch
Fair Amoret—the Maid was *rich*.

LVI.

Oft had he tried the walls of gold
That held in thraldom his desire;
But when he neared the enchanted hold,
Then hideous sulphur, smoke, and fire,*
Against him from the porch were rolled,
And forced him desperate to retire;
At length the venture he gave o'er,
As did the bold Sir Scudamour.

LVII.

Now, entering by his drowsy head,
The Dream Ambassador stood fast:
"Why sigh you so, fair Sir," he said,
"For buried glories of the past,
Deeming that Chivalry is dead,
When Heaven adventure sows broadcast?
In vain the blessed Gods are kind
To mortals' prayers, if men be blind.

---

* "No gate they found them to withhold,
  Nor ward to wait at morne and evening late,
  But in the porch that did them soon amate,
  A flaming fire, ymixt with smouldry smoke,
  And stinking sulphure, that with griesly hate
  And dreadful horror did all entraunce choke,
  And forced them their forward footing to revoke."
                    SPENSER'S *Faery Queen*, 3, 11, 21.

LVIII.

"True knighthood springs from knightly brain,
  And had mankind but souls to see,
Deeds, more than all that poets feign,
  Or fancy fables, now might be;
Love should be Law, and Honour reign,
  Queens should wed Squires of low degree,
Wit make a way where wealth deters,
And Valour win the golden Spurs.

LIX.

"O days when Love made Woman wise,
  When, veiling all her maiden mien,
She fought with men in man's disguise!
  Think, if in fight her face was seen,
How from their eyes, by sweet surprise,
  Must Love like light have sprung between!
Ah! were those maids but modern men,
Knighthood! thou shouldst return again.

LX.

For see! What things do Women dare!
  How maids eclipse their knightly noon!
Man's company they quite forswear,
  And seek a cloister in the Moon.
Well may bold Celia scorn the prayer
  Of craven lovers, she, who soon,
Scot free from Gravity's restraints,
Will fly where your weak Fancy faints.

LXI.

" Once led by Love to seek her mate,
  A maid from Giants won renown,
Nor fainted 'neath her armour's weight;
  But you, you fear a woman's frown!
The hold you dread 's a College gate!
  The armour you decline, the gown!
And now Occasion might secure
Your dreams, you, valiant Knight, are poor!

LXII.

" Poor, when Adventure calls! 'Tis well!
  Poor, when the Gods are on your side!
Know, in the Moon the Immortals dwell,
  And scorn by maids to be defied.
Now Venus sets you in her selle,
  And bids you lower a damsel's pride.
Fair Celia's conqueror! Venus' Knight!
Go forth! and Love defend the Right."

LXIII.

He said: and with two bright moonbeams
  Transfixed his heart; then swiftly flies;
But up sprang Amadis; he deems
  His garret Elf-land; in his eyes
The soul of gowned Achilles gleams;
  Memory and Hope of new emprise
His bosom fire; unwonted arms
At once he seeks, and woman's charms.

LXIV.

Smooth was his cheek, and clear his eye;
Myrtillo's self he might have been,
Who mixed with maids in Arcady;
Or his the young Diego's mien,
Who for sweet voice and fair reply
Was crowned those merry ladies' Queen,
Who feasted in the sculptor's home
Under the jasmin bowers in Rome.*

LXV.

Soon ribbed in iron like the fair,
Wide satin folds his footsteps trammel;
Clad in the arms that women wear,
Well-pencilled eyebrows, smooth enamel,
And nodding helmet of brown hair,
He stands a *sans reproche*—Belle Brummel:
Then all on high adventure bent,
With Hope and Morning forth he went.

LXVI.

Now to the hold, whose walls immure
His Celia, Love our Knight has led;
Broad was the Gate and barred secure;
High o'er the arch a Sculpture dread

---

* "Era ivi per ispalliera alle donne un tessuto di gelsumini naturali e bellissimi, il quale faceva tanto bel campo a quelle donne che impossibile saria il dirlo con parole."—*Vita di Benvenuto Cellini*, libro i. cap. 30.

Stood from a broad entablature,
Queen Tomyris holding Cyrus' head,*
Whereby to males was clearly bruited
All trespass would be prosecuted.

LXVII.

But neither Death nor fear of it
Deterred the youth, but grace divine
Inspired his soul with Woman's wit,
And thus he prayed with deep design:
" Open, sweet Ladies, and admit
A damsel, lover of Moonshine,
Who to your happy Hall is driven
By hate of man, and hope of Heaven."

LXVIII.

Within Cornelia heard the sound.
Like old Cyrene she was sitting
With circles of fair maidens crowned,—
Yet half this simile's unfitting:
'Tis true sweet gossip went the round,
But sometimes flagged for lack of knitting;
For woman's idle Genius lingers
Most kindly where she's busy fingers.†

---

* "ἀσκὸν δὲ πλήσασα αἵματος ἀνθρωπηΐου Τόμυρις, ἐδίζητο ἐν τοῖσι τεθνεῶσι τῶν Περσέων τὸν Κύρου νέκυν, ὡς δὲ εὗρε ἐναπῆπτε αὐτοῦ τὴν κεφαλὴν ἐς τὸν ἀσκόν."

"Having filled a skin with human blood, Tomyris searched among the Persian dead for the body of Cyrus, and when she found it she fastened up his head in the skin."—HERODOTUS: *Clio*, 214.

† At any rate Virgil seems to have thought so, judging from his

LXIX.

Round them the grey quadrangle made
The green grass brighter in the sun,
Where, in the midst, a fountain played,
Clear-toned as Mercury's silver run—
Mercury, above whose nightly shade
Tom beats his hundred strokes and one.*
But ah! what Nereids crowned that fount
He must be Virgil who could count.

LXX.

There, with their white necks veiled in hair,†
Sat Mabels, Margarets, Mauds, and Maries,
Ethel and Blanche—sea-bathing pair,
Who at Llandudno 'd left their Lares—

---

pretty picture of Cyrene and her nymphs, sitting under the river, working, and telling stories :—

    "At mater sonitum thalamo sub fluminis alti
    Sensit. Eam circum Milesia vellera nymphæ
    Carpebant, hyali saturo fucata colore.
    *   *   *   *
    Inter quas curam Clymene narrabat inanem
    Vulcani," &c.   VIRG. : *Georg.* iv. 333.

* Mercury, the fountain in Tom Quadrangle, Christchurch, Oxford. Tom sounds one hundred and one strokes (the number of the Ch. Ch. students) at nine o'clock every night—the signal for closing the College gates.

† "Drymoque, Xanthoque, Ligeaque, Phyllodoceque,
    Cæsariem effusæ nitidam per candida colla ;
    Nisæe Spioque, Thaliaque, Cymodoceque,
    Cydippeque, et flava Lycorias : altera virgo,
    Altera tum primos Lucinæ experta labores ;

Lucia for love of pug-dogs fair
Renowned, and Cynthia of canaries,
And last the maiden archer's pride,
Rose, with her arrows laid aside.

LXXI.

In the clear wave, with sleeves up-rolled,
White arms and jewelled fingers gleam;
The fountain felt so fresh and cold,
The falling water made them dream;
Meantime the wise Cornelia told
A tale of science and of steam,
When the clear summons made them start:
Flushed every cheek, and leapt each heart.

LXXII.

The soft entreaty heard once more,
Rose, fairest portress of the gaol,
Unbarred in haste the College door,
And brought the youth within the pale:
So strange a novice ne'er before,
To nunnery bound and maiden veil,
Was let within a cloistered wall
By half so sweet a seneschal.

Clioque et Beroë soror, Oceanitides ambæ,
Ambæ auro, pictis incinctæ pellibus ambæ;
Atque Ephyre, atque Opis, atque Asia Deïopea,
Et tandem positis velox Arethusa sagittis."

VIRG.: *Georg.* iv. 336.

LXXIII.

But as the Trojan in the Shades
Was all beset with Ghosts forlorn ;*
So pressed the fair and learned maids
Round this new traveller to their bourne :
Tidings they asked of lace and braids,
How boots were heeled, what skirts were worn,
What hair was favourite, blonde or brown,
And what the latest match in town.

LXXIV.

But he shut in by fluttering choirs,
Fanned by the soft wind of their dresses,
With rapt and silent soul admires
Star-hosts of eyes and meteor tresses ;
Gathers their thoughts from their attires,
And from their looks their natures guesses ;
At length before Cornelia brought,
His errand the Queen-Blue besought.

LXXV.

Blushing his ardour to reveal,
The Star, he answered, of her fame
Led him, and love of woman's weal,
And Amaryllis was his name.

---

* " Circumstant animæ dextra lævaque frequentes.
  Nec vidisse semel satis est ; juvat usque morari,
  Et conferre gradum, et veniendi discere causas."
  VIRG. : Æn. vi. 486.

Pleased with this show of maiden zeal,
And by the flattery touched, the Dame
Makes haste to grant the wished-for boon,—
Matriculation for the Moon.

LXXVI.

At once a beauteous eager crew
A gown of softest silk prepare,
And hood from Oxford stol'n, the Blue
That Bachelors of Medicine wear,
('Twas judged by all the prettiest hue);
With trencher cap they crown his hair,
Then on her Book, he nothing loath,
Cornelia swears him in by oath.

LXXVII.

"O Amaryllis, will you here,
　Leaving all follies, study till
Arcs, rhomboids, gnomons, are made clear?"
　Said Amadis, "With my poor skill."
"Will you love, cherish, and hold dear
　Our sex alone?" Said he, "I will."
"And swear no tyrant's ring to wear
　As wedded wife?" Said he, "I swear."

BOOK III.

ARGUMENT.

CORNELIA, betaking herself on a summer day to her lawn, reads treatises to her College on the Art of Moonflying, but the Assembly seeming absent and abstracted, Sibylla declares that Love has equipped one of the number with powers of sorcery, and proposes to discover the witch by the ordeal of the kiss. Amaryllis, as the latest comer and the most innocent, is chosen from the rest, who are commanded by Sibylla to kiss her in turn, which, being duly done, Celia is pronounced guilty, and is fined. At nightfall Amaryllis betakes herself to the window of Celia, and after an argument concerning Love and Knowledge, tells the story of Endymion and the Moon, at the close of which her sex is accidentally revealed to Celia by the loss of her chignon. Meantime, Pyrrha, one of the College, being unable to rest, has wandered by herself upon the lawn to meditate on the sweet remembrance of Amaryllis' kiss, and, unperceived, comes suddenly upon Amaryllis and Celia. Fired by jealousy and patriotism, she rouses the sleeping College, who surround the lovers. Amadis declares his willingness to die, but avows that his enterprise was prompted by the Gods, and warns the Women against their impious attempt upon the Moon. Cornelia, hurling defiance against the Gods, challenges them to battle in the air on the following night.

BOOK III.

I.

O COURTEOUS ladies, kind and fair,
Who travel patient with my tale,
And, borne with me from earth and air,
Passing beneath the Muses' veil,
Have seen what plots the Gods prepare
In the far realms of Moonshine pale,
Descend awhile to Earth, and hear
How now they prospered in our sphere.

II.

For thus, O ladies, you, who fence
Your hearts in unbelief, or you,
Who deem my gods a light pretence,
Veiled as they are from mortal view,
You shall have proof by earthly sense
That all my tale of Heaven is true,
And learn what influences unseen
Move in your bosoms joy and teen.

III.

Then, Muse, wherever thou art strayed,
Learned in the lover's ancient art,
Return, and tell how every maid,
Whom Love had wounded with his dart,
Was languishing; how oft they bade
Defiance to the treacherous heart,
Yet, traitors still, whole hours would steal
From knowledge, since they learned to feel.

IV.

For sometimes through their faces, free,
Ran the red tide; the sudden sigh
Was heard at lecture; you might see
The restless start, the dreaming eye:
Deep in their bosoms curiously
Small golden hearts lay nestling shy.
And now in course of time the moon
Had well nigh filled her horns in June.

V.

Upon a day it came to pass,
Moved by the Summer and the Sun,
Cornelia, on the soft green grass
Sat with her maidens every one
(So the decree of Venus was)
Spite of herself her heart was won,
For now old memories made her grieve
For the warm earth she meant to leave.

VI.

But prudent still, though yielding thus,
She read from many an antique page
Of magic arts, unknown to us ;
Of alchemist, and soaring sage ;
Much pondering now on Icarus,
Now on the wings of Simon Mage,
And Alexander's* crafts that come
Through Cagliostro down to Home.

VII.

But sometimes, pausing in suspense,
She saw her maidens listless lying,
And in their eyes the wandering sense
Of Thought in worlds of Fancy dying,
Or now some soul re-travelling thence,
With conscious look to look replying,
As travellers, met abroad, re-meet
At home, with glances in the street.

VIII.

One, on her white arm firmly leaned,
Sank in her muslin-mantled breast
Her dreaming head ; another screened
The features that her soul confessed ;
And this, with fancies all convened,
Upon a neighbouring shoulder pressed
Her forehead, hoping with dark eyes
Sweet thoughts in ambush to surprise.

---

* See Lucian's account of this ancient Spiritualist.

IX.

Then cried the Prophetess, "Ah me!
Those lightning barbs in poison dipt
Have then struck home! now this is He
Whom lately on this lawn we whipt.
With charms of idle sorcery
One of these maids hath he equipt,
Who with wild thoughts, though unexpressed,
Hath wickedly bewitched the rest.

X.

" Men needed once by test of fire
To try the sorceress: limb from limb
They tore her; nay, the Southern Shire
Would prove her still by 'sink or swim.'
Such judgments little I require;
That maid, who's sold her soul to Him,
Shall be approved, like all that's His,
By the great ordeal of the Kiss.

XI.

"Sweet Amaryllis! well I know *
Your heart by Love is still untried,
Who felt not as did these his bow;
Now seat you on this green bankside:

---

* Every one, who knows Guarini's Pastor Fido, will see that I have adapted the pretty scene of Myrtillo and Amaryllis, in Act 2, S. 1. In justice to myself I give a sketch of the original, to show that I am rather a debtor than a thief. Myrtillo relates how he was introduced by his sister, in the dress of a woman, into the company of Amaryllis and her friends, and how one of the latter proposed a kind of Olympic game of kissing, how Amaryllis was elected judge, and how, after all

Each maid shall on your lips bestow
A kiss, and I for all decide;
For she who hides this guilt shall speak
By red confession of her cheek."

XII.

With secret joy the maids comply,
Yet feared; so strangely sweet it seemed
To kiss, so deeply came the sigh:
Each cheek with brighter crimson gleamed:
And this they knew, but knew not why,
Nor if they waked, nor if they dreamed.
Thus they by Amaryllis passed,
And kissed her: Celia was the last.

XIII.

And all beheld with more delight
Her supple limbs in her white gown
Bow, like a lily from its height,
The blonde hair mingling with the brown;
But none could see the long, long light
Of looks that met as she bent down,
Light that drew thought into eclipse,
And made life linger on the lips.*

---

had kissed her, she decided that the most lover-like kiss had been given by Myrtillo. There is no prettier passage of artificial simplicity in any literature.

* " Su queste labbra, Ergasto,
    Tutta sen venne allor l'anima mia,
    E la mia vita chiusa
    In cosi breve spazio
    Non er' altro che un bacio."

XIV.

But as some white anemone,
Whence honey thieves her sweetness hale,
Losing the burden of the bee,
Sways to and fro as in a gale ;
So Celia rose, so trembled she,
With changing cheek now red, now pale,
Convicted by some power unknown
Of crimes her conscience must disown.

XV.

With joy the Sibyl hailed the clue ;
'Tis vain for Celia to protest ;
Still, so she swore, an honest Blue,
Good Euclid's shrine was in her breast ;
Her eye proclaimed her oath untrue ;
Her convict cheek the crime confessed ;
Each maiden hypocrite her head
Averts, and thus Cornelia said :

XVI.

"My sister, those who greatly stray
Must look for retribution great ;
Two pairs of eyebrows you will pay,
A patch and paint-brush to the State ;
The three first books of Euclid say
By heart, and keep within the gate :
So recognize, ye maids, what awe,
Sanctions the majesty of Law !"

XVII.

The girls their reverent heads incline,
But whisperingly the thing repeat;
Some think that, if the sorceress' fine
Were heavy, yet the sin was sweet;
Some, too, their Celia's thoughts divine,
So strange, so *very* indiscreet;
The rest fetch task-books, and obey
The Queen's partition of the day.

XVIII.

And now 'twas night—ah! such a night,
As seems so still in man's repose,
That from the very jasmins white
A kind of silent language goes,
And Time by lilies in moonlight
Lies sleeping, or beside the rose,
Till waked with dawn, the sudden comer,
He lift his lids, and greet—Midsummer.

XIX.

A night when daylight seems to last,
Yet sounder sleeps the roof-lodged swallow;
When all the flowers deep shadows cast,
And each holds moonshine in its hollow;
A night when everything that's past
Is beautiful, and all to follow
Looks sweetly dim and softly bright;
So still, so fragrant was the night.

XX.

Such night young Romeo's loves began
With Juliet, and Lorenzo gay
Through the melodious changes ran
"On such a night" with Jessica;
Then since on such the maiden-man,
Our Amaryllis, chose to stray
Within the garden,—who can blame
If he to Celia's window came?

XXI.

Three stories high was built the hall,
And on the lowest was her chamber.
All round the grey-stone moonlit wall
He saw the stealthy roses clamber,
And jasmin o'er the casement fall;
And soon a little lamp like amber
Revealed the maiden, as she came
A picture moving in its frame.

XXII.

Now thus surprised in secret mood
A woman true was Celia shown;
For, if 'tis fear of solitude,
Or to self-knowledge they are prone,
All womankind, coquette or prude,
Whene'er they find themselves alone,
(Or think they are,) directly pass
To seek for friendship in their glass.

XXIII.

But sure of glasses never one,
Since Pope made rhymes and Steele wrote essays,
Had shown a face like this fair nun,
Or held such length of shining tresses,
Wherein by turns her brushes run,
Like boats in western wildernesses,
That sometimes shoot the rapid's tide,
And sometimes in the rushes hide.

XXIV.

As where the Goddess' temple shone
At lamplight in the Cyprian water,
The priestess, when the world was gone,
Would turn to see the gifts they brought her
From Ophir or from Lebanon;
So Celia, being Eve's true daughter,
Now turned in secret to behold
Her lockets and her rings of gold.

XXV.

Caught with the colour, now she sets
The scarlet coral in her head;
Now, in a dream, her hand forgets
What it desired; her neck is spread
With chains and little amulets;
On her white breast a ruby red
Lies, crimson, as a blood-stain glows
From leveret struck in Alpine snows.

XXVI.

But as she stood her upper gown
Like silent snow-stream downward slipped ;
Then with hot cheek, and smile, and frown,
Her round white shoulder's linen crypt
She pressed,—so doves in their own down
Will nestle—and, half open lipped,
Kissed it, as though, like that poor elf,
She'd play Narcissus to herself.

XXVII.

" Ah me ! " she cries, " what ails my breast ?
For since that little wanton boy
I found asleep, I have no rest,
Nor books, nor learning, I enjoy ;
O Celia ! falcon in dove's nest !
Helen in my Cornelia's Troy !
Yet if I could, would I forego
This sin ? Alas, I hardly know—

XXVIII.

" Is it a sin ? The stars above
Make me for Amaryllis sigh ;
Else why should breath, and touch, and glove,
Move you, my heart ? ah, tell me why ?
Can ever woman woman love ?
This Sappho did—then so might I ;
Or rather is't some face like hers,
That me to love by proxy stirs ?

XXIX.

" If Amadis "—therewith there came
  A little pebble, aimed full featly
Against the glass, and she for shame
  Blushed red, as one who indiscreetly
Has told her friends her lover's name;
  Then to the window ran she fleetly,
And with half-glad, half-guilty scream,
Beheld the author of her dream.

XXX.

Yet feigning still the Scholar's cue,
" Did not," she cries, " our Legislator
  Swear us to Knowledge to be true?
Then, why this perjury? Idle traitor!
  Go! ponder on the cause of dew!
Incline the Sun to the Equator!
  Or do for some one of the Stars
The kindness Kepler did for Mars!"

XXXI.

Then Amaryllis: " Ah, unkind!
  Not mine to Knowledge is the treason
But yours to Nature: 'tis divined
  By some our Souls obey the season,
And as Heaven's influences bind
  Our thoughts from morn till eve by Reason
So, when the Stars are seen above,
They set our spirits free by Love."

XXXII.

Then with a shudder Celia : " Hush !
Name not a name of such ill omen,
Lest in the dark he make us blush ;
We are the monster's natural foemen ;
Power he may have o'er men ; but, tush !
Not Love but Knowledge rules o'er women ;
Eden for her was lost by Eve ;
Eden by Knowledge we'll retrieve.

XXXIII.

" You know we hope by Knowledge soon
Disease and death from Earth to scare,
And each, a self-propelled balloon,—
What broomstick witches used to dare—
To mount for rambles in the Moon,
Although they say it has no air,
Nay, if it please us, take a pattern
For targets from the rings of Saturn."

XXXIV.

Said he : " And if you did, with ease
Love would pursue you to those parts ;
Deeper than Knowledge in the seas
He dives, much deeper in men's hearts ;
Knowledge may master Sciences,
But Love is Bachelor of Arts ;
Knowledge shows laws but cannot give,
Love is his own Executive.

XXXV.

"Full oft, like a small watchman, he,
  With hood and lantern armed, comes creeping
'Neath mortal eaves, where fancy free
  The maidens and young men lie sleeping;
Then with his lips, as with a key,
  He steals their hearts out of their keeping,
And they, like changelings of the elves,
Awake, and fear, and doubt themselves.

XXXVI.

"But Knowledge, throned in her cold star,
  Sits pinched and cruel as an ogress,
Therefore is Love the stronger far;
  And though our trade is blessed by Progress,
Think you our hearts much wiser are
  Than Knights of Lyonesse and Logres?
Or say you that our Savans' rods
Should whip the old poets for their Gods?"

XXXVII.

Said she: "In Love you seem no dunce,
  While we are but two girls at play;
But if some man came all at once
  You'd have no syllable to say:
Or come, forget your frill and flounce—
  I had a lover on my day,
(Ah may my penitence undo
My crime!) in part resembling you.

XXXVIII.

" Now leave those maiden looks demure,
And play like him the man, or goose,
And woo me, Love, as Queen Budoor
Once wooed Queen Hayet El Nufoos;
So will I give you proof how poor
A lord is Love—for I'll reduce
His syllogisms to powdered cocoa,
Either in Barbara or Baroko.*

XXXIX.

" I dare, I dare you, amorous maid!
Now let not Love your heart attaint,
As a mere braggart in his trade "—
But then, compelled by sweet constraint
To beg as bounty what she bade,
And with the odorous time grown faint,
Her bosom and her cheek she pressed,
Softly, on Amaryllis' breast.

---

* Women, it seems, are at last to learn logic. But, O fair and gentle ladies, have you any conception of the rigmarole you must acquire before you can cure yourselves of your charming habit of arguing in a circle? Let the poet Aldrich recount to you the figures:—

" *Barbara, Celarent, Darii, Ferioque,* prioris;
Cesare, Camestres, Festino, Baroko, secundæ;
Tertia, *Darapti, Disamis, Datisi, Felapton,*
Bokardo, Ferison habet: Quarta insuper addit
Bramantip, Camenes, Dimaris, Fesapo, Fresison,
Quinque *Subalterni* totidem *Generalibus* orti,
Nomen habent nullum, nec si *bene colligis* usum."

XL.

And while the chesnut and the lime
Made shadows quaint on lawn and gravel,
Which seemed like quiet Inns for Time
After the heat of his day's travel,
Said she: "Since Love, and Stars, and Rhyme,
Can read what Reason can't unravel,
Come tell me to some pretty tune
The secret meaning of the Moon.

XLI.

"For though our telescopes by night
Her hills and valleys now discover,
Did not some old and foolish wight
Fancy the Moon was once true Lover?"
Then he, who, worshipping Moonlight,
Through all Romanceland had been rover,
Thus in his northern tongue essayed
The myth that sweet Tassoni made.

XLII.

"In herbs and flowers Endymion slept,*
Tired with the labour of the day:
The Summer and the Twilight kept
Around him cool and amorous play;

---

* I give here (*pace* Mr. Max Müller and the Sun and the Dawn) one of those myths which modern "Science" has branded as "a conglomeration of meaningless and absurd stories," a translation of the Song of Scarpinello, in "La Secchia Rapita," praised by Alfieri as one of the wonders of Italian poetry. I cannot pretend to approach the original,

The little Loves, like squires adept,
His arrows took, for as he lay
With fair closed eyelids on the grass,
They thought that he Lord Cupid was.

XLIII.

"A passing wind across his face,
In showers of gold his tresses blew;
The Loves ran up, and in their place
Set them all back in order due;
And flowers they picked, and wove apace
Crowns for his head of various hue,
And chains his arms and feet to deck,
And collars for his snowy neck.

XLIV.

"To match his amorous lips they seek
What red the peony can boast,
And rose and lily for his cheek;
But peony, rose, lily lost.
The wind and wave kept silence meek;
No murmur o'er the hillside crossed,
Each in his tongue, earth, air, and deep,
Seemed to say, "Hush! 'tis Love asleep!"

---

for the sweetness of their language, so suggestive of irony, gives the burlesque-writers of Italy an advantage over those of every other nation. But I have adhered throughout to the spirit of the poet, and generally to his text, except where I saw that an alteration would be better adapted to the character of an English style.

XLV.

"As in Heaven field, where the great Bull
Flames through the splendour of the night,
Those Sister Stars, so clear and full,
That daughters of old Atlas hight,
Round her, that is most beautiful
And largest, shine, less fair yet bright,
So with the Loves appeared in worth
Endymion in the flowers of Earth.

XLVI.

"When she who rules in Heaven's first ring,
Bright with the Sun's departed rays,
The world's dark stage uncurtaining,
The lonely silent lands surveys,
Dews from her mantle scattering
And rime upon the flowery ways,
By chance she spied this hill, then she
Came down from Heaven all curiously.

XLVII.

"The Loves beheld and feared, and thence
They fled; but she, when on the hill
She saw him sleep, with maiden sense,
Gazing, on balanced foot stood still,
And kept from Love in sweet suspense
Of modesty and fear of ill,
She had half turned to flee, but then
His fair face called her back again.

XLVIII.

"So through her eyes her heart took fire,
  Which Love made master of her Soul;
Little by little, with desire,
  Towards the sleeping boy she stole;
And of the flowrets, which the choir
  Had woven in thousand fashions droll,
She made her brow and bosom rings:
But ah! each flower had flames and stings!

XLIX.

"Flowers drew her hand, her hand the kiss
  Drew to eyes, cheek, mouth, bosom white;
So lively, and so long to his
  Her lips were pressed, that with affright
He woke, and now, for fear of this
  Illumined world so heavenly bright,
He would adown the rocks have leapt,
But him she caught and straitly kept.

L.

"'O sweet and sleepy Soul,' she said,
  'What do you fear? I am the Moon,
Who now to sleep with you am led
  By Love, and Fate, and Fortune's boon.
Sit down and rest. Be comforted;
  And while the night is yet in noon,
Choose now this love that I reveal
To hide, or else Heaven's wrath to feel!'

LI.

"'Eye of the world! Lady of Dew!
A shepherd lad that keep poor kine
Am I,' he said; 'but now would you
Take me to Heaven by grace divine,
Doubt not I shall be always true;
And this white robe, to be a sign,
Which Etlius gave, for his love's sake,
To Calice, my mother, take.'

LII.

"With that his scarf, which daintily
Was fringed with pearls, and so was tied
That back and breast as one might be
From the right shoulder to left side,
He gave her as a gift. Then she
Quite lost in love her heavenly pride;
And as a flower, pressed on its bank,
Droops faintly, in his arms she sank.

LIII.

"Not in such close embrace the vine
The elm her fruitless husband presses,
Nor ivy round the shady pine
So tightly wreathes her winding tresses,
As did these lovers' arms entwine
Each other in their long caresses,
The while their lips shot arrows sweet,
That Love on his own anvil beat.

LIV.

"Thus while, in Cupid's courtesies
 Looks, kisses, sighs, embraces using,
They play such follies as seem wise
 Only by happy lovers' choosing,
The Goddess lifted her bright eyes,
 The elements and stars accusing
That she, made blind by powers above,
So long had followed beasts not Love.

LV.

"'Ah!' cried she, 'how I erred that day
 I took the bow, and tracked the wood!
What years since then have slipped away,
 That now I never can make good!
O life of which the winds made play!
 So wandering! so misunderstood!
How much more sweet had been this fruit
Than dangers dared in vain pursuit!

LVI.

"'I see my fault, and I would fain
 Atone, but Heaven will not consent;
And for the future but remain
 Resolves I never shall repent.
Hear, therefore, Earth, and Air, and Main,
 What I propose with fixed intent;
And let this law for ever bind
Obedient me and womankind:

LVII.

"' For I decree for future doom
    The sky I rule no maid shall cover,
(Save some few ugly spinsters, whom
    Nor I, nor any star reign over,)
Who shall be rebel till the tomb,
    And close her heart to every lover;
But she, that holds love's passion light,
Deceives, or does herself despite.'"

LVIII.

Then how the Goddess to her sphere
    Returned in grief, he would have told;
But Celia, to whose English ear
    The song though sweet seemed somewhat bold,
(O women! priests and insincere!
    Who wait for "Finis" ere ye scold;
'Tis thus that Mrs. Grundy's law
Ye sanction!*) Celia moved and saw—

LIX.

Where were ye, Sylphs aërial, where?
    Why so securely did ye roam,

---

* Let the Prophets of Progress and Perfection say, if this epigram is not as true in our own enlightened era as in the bad times of Domitian and Martial:—

    "Erubuit, posuitque meum Lucretia librum;
        Sed coram Bruto. Brute, recede; leget."

Who made Belinda's lock your care,
And in false ringlets have your home?
Did ye by moonlight chase the hair,
Or shell the tortoise for the comb,
That careless of your fair dominion
Ye watched not Amaryllis' chignon?

LX.

Now tell me, all ye maiden squires,
Who tend fair dame on nightly field,
What secret clasp, what hidden wires,
What whalebone light, or pin concealed,
Rivets that helmet which attires
Their heads,—and now the youth revealed;
Then will I match his Faery art,
Who once unhelmed maid Britomart.*

LXI.

But O sweet Celia! who can write
What moved your bosom, girlish Fear,
Or Fancy, or a girl's delight
In Frolic, dread of tongues severe,
The tale, the silence, and the night,
And Love the blind, and Love the seer?
This, this could any poet do,
Methinks it were a girl like you.

---

* See the beautiful description of Britomart unhelmed. *Faery Queen*, 4, 6, 19, 20.

LXII.

And surely now had Love been lord,
And Venus won the doubtful game,
When Chance, dark deity, abhorred
By gods and men, who loves to unframe
All fair designs, beheld the board,
And spoiled the wily goddess' aim;
For, seeing Cornelia's hand withdrawn,
Herself by proxy played a pawn.

LXIII.

There was a girl among the rest
Named Pyrrha, one of sisters three,
Whose names their natures well expressed,
Light Lesbia, laughing Lalage;
Thereby, too, Pyrrha stood confessed,
Stormy and shifting as the sea,
Whose passions changed in strong desire,
Like Proteus, to wind, wave, or fire.

LXIV.

Love all his deadliest shafts at her
Had shot; no arrow seemed to miss:
Save Celia's self, none livelier
Had felt the magic of the Kiss;
And this, her passions all astir,
With joy and pain reviving, this
To reimagine, she'd withdrawn
By moonlight on the silent lawn.

LXV.

And as some Bacchanal in Thrace,
Her naked feet with swiftness shod,
Leaving her comrades in the race,
Would halt on snows before untrod,
And lifting to the stars her face
Deep in her bosom felt the god,
So Pyrrha's heart beneath her zone
Now bounds with power beyond its own.

LXVI.

One while upon her bosom white
Her bodkin's silver point she drives;
The small red stain in the moonlight
The memory of Love's barb revives:
Then in rapt colloquy with night,
" Tell me," she cried, " ye wedded wives,
Ye that have either state essayed,
If maiden's love suffice for maid!"

LXVII.

But when no answer came, instead,
" O Night, and flowers with dew-drops pearled,
If in your still white cups," she said,
" As some believe, soft wings are furled,
Souls of old lovers long time dead,
Who once took pleasure in this world,
To one, who breathes in pain above,
Now speak, and say, Does Pyrrha love?"

LXVIII.

For Amaryllis' chamber light
She looked, but when no radiance shone,
" O spirit innocent and white,"
She said, " to Dreamland you are gone!
You know not Pyrrha's wretched plight,
Caused by your kiss, nor dream thereon,
Else you, like me, should vigil keep,
And Love should be your lord, not Sleep."

LXIX.

Just as she spoke, the moon's soft glow,
On the quadrangle brightly shining,
Showed her two girls, or seemed to show,
Leaned lover-like with arms entwining;
One spoke caressingly and low,
And one was on her breast reclining.
Heavens! sees she in a rival's fane
The goddess of her love and pain?

LXX.

She strains her eyes, doubts, disbelieves,
While with mixed passions blindly swayed
Her breast tempestuously heaves;
She steals from silent shade to shade,
Crossing bright spaces 'neath the leaves,
As to Venetian serenade
The husband steals like statue mute,
Tracking the lover by his lute.

LXXI.

She sees them separate, then again
Return; she breathes their mingling breath;
To fancy this had been sweet pain,
But so to feel, poor child! was death:
"This bold girl gallant to disdain—!"
Her bodkin from its velvet sheath
She took, but as she nearer stole
An instant glance revealed the whole.

LXXII.

How weak are mortals, even the wise!
How are we blinded by extremes!
How passion makes our being rise
Till every fault a virtue seems!
Pyrrha beheld, and from her eyes
A storm of outraged Honour gleams,
While ecstasy of private Hate
Makes her a lover of the State.

LXXIII.

The Hall in swift and silent course
She reached (her feet her soul obeyed);
And through the sleeping corridors,
"Wake, wake!" she cries, "we are betrayed!
Up, Sisters! to the danger's source!
Celia the witch, and the false maid!
'Tis hence these sorceries all began;
FOR AMARYLLIS IS A MAN."

LXXIV.

As when upon Cithæron's shrine,
The Mænad matrons, worshipping,
Heard suddenly the voice divine
Through all the silent spaces ring,
And, gazing upwards through the pine,
Beheld the petticoated King:*
So Pyrrha's anguished cry pierced deep
The souls of maidens in their sleep.

LXXV.

Ah! were this pen a painter's brush!
For, roused as by a peal of thunder,
Up sprang the girls with sleep's sweet flush
Still on their cheeks, and eyes of wonder;
What snowy night-robes swelled the rush!
And ah! what white feet gleamed thereunder!
So fluttered by some late affright,
The dovecote makes the darkness white.

LXXVI.

But now poor Pyrrha's tale is told,
Now are the luckless lovers found.
Then, as some robber of the fold,
Whom all the village hinds impound,
But none to brave his claws makes bold,
All wisely valiant stand around:
So round the youth the ring expands,
And he at bay, the lion, stands.

---

* See EURIPIDES: *Bacchæ*, 1073.

LXXVII.

Ye gods, what Thoughts, and in what guise,
Went travelling to your lunar seat?
What Whims, Desires, and Jealousies,
What Jesuit Fancies, veiled, discreet?
Poor Celia stands with downcast eyes,
And fathoms her own heart's deceit:
Just now her love, with place and time,
Was joy—made public, 'tis a crime.

LXXVIII.

Then, to the maidens, Amadis:
" Ladies, if death be your decree
For those that dare your lips to kiss,
Well. Such was life enough for me.
But this maid's heart did nought amiss;
Then leave her, like her conscience, free.
Nay, hope you aught from death like mine,
'Tis vain; you war with powers divine.

LXXIX.

" O fellow mortals, let me plead.
Ye know that, from our earliest hours,
We're but Heaven's sport, and in each deed
Nought but the empty act is ours;
The wish, the thought are both decreed
By Parliament of Heavenly powers;
Our hearts as in the wind they bow,
And shape desire we know not how.

LXXX.

" Thus to your college was I led :
    A wingèd Dream from Heaven came down,
    And o'er my soul bright fancies shed,
    Arraying me in woman's gown ;
    Love's mighty Empress, so he said,
    Would here my bold adventure crown ;
    Then how ye sought the Moon he showed :
' That is,' said he, ' the Gods' abode.'

LXXXI.

" Methinks the lords of mortal hearts
    Thought scorn to see their vassals bold
    Profane in thought their sacred parts,
    And wake their starry silence old.
    Theirs were these counsels, theirs these arts ;
    Me but as conscript they enrolled.
    If I as man may not be shriven,
    Surely some grace is due to Heaven."

LXXXII.

He ceased, for all the maids he saw
    Tremble with terror and surprise :
    With upward glance of timorous awe
    They scan the moon and starry skies :
    Not so Cornelia. Looking law
    And judgment from majestic eyes,
    (Through spectacles) papyrus-curled,
    She fronts the old rulers of the world.

LXXXIII.

"Misguided youth," she said, "and you,
  O maid (if that shame-mantled cheek
  Still shows the Celia whom I knew),
  In vain deliverance hence you seek.
  Heaven has no terrors for a Blue.
  Your champions like yourselves are weak."
Then, with her clenched hands towering high,
  She hurls defiance to the sky.

LXXXIV.

"Hence, then, these efforts of the Gods!
  These battles, marches, sallies, raids,
  This twilight strife with open odds,
  These thievish midnight ambuscades!
  For this, O Love, you braved our rods,
  To shoot your arrows at the maids!
  For this in secret mined our laws!
  Your plots I saw, but not the cause.

LXXXV.

"For never yet did sage's glass
  Find mark of Heaven in yon bright sign,
  Where never motion seemed to pass,
  Darkening the clear and silent shine;
  Of hill and dale, of gold and brass,
  Our souls had dreamed, but nought divine;
  So far, worn exiles, did ye fly,
  From Science and wise woman's eye.

LXXXVI.

" I thought from your old mount expelled,
    Driven like pale ghosts on wave and wind,
Full of all penury and eld,
    Ye wandered weary through mankind ;
Or haply some fool's fancy held,
    Some poet's heart, some childish mind ;
Lo ! now enthroned on lunar heights,
I find you foes to Woman's Rights.

LXXXVII.

" Twice bold ! twice baffled and outcast !
    Kings of an old forgotten reign !
Gods of the passions of the Past !
    Behold this night your arts how vain !
Art not thou vanquished, Love, at last ?
    Or wilt thou tempt the maids again ?
Yet as ye will, come one, come all,
Each time ye come, ye come to fall.

LXXXVIII.

" Because the same bright sun shines down,
    And the same stars their vigils keep ;
Because the snows the mountains crown,
    And rivers run into the deep ;
Because, through country-side and town,
    Hunger is lord, and Death and Sleep :
Think you we women are like those
Ye sought from old Olympus' snows ?'

LXXXIX.

"O fools and blind!   The red French flood
  Has washed the old world's dotage young;
And Pyrrha, rebaptized in blood,*
  Is now on earth regenerate sprung.
The landmarks of old womanhood
  Are lost, her images down-flung:
For all brute passions of the slave
Lie with dead tyrants in the grave.

XC.

"Old lords of Custom, ye have seen
  A hundred generations die,
As leaves in lustihead of green
  When winds of Autumn whirl them by;
Behold, I say, *ye too have been ;*
  Use and Prescription—these must die.
Olympus ye have lost, and soon
Shall show your title to the Moon.

XCI.

Hope nought from Privilege; nor boast
  The safety of your island Star,
Since space divides you from our coast:—
  No world for mortals is too far.†

---

* The first Pyrrha was wife of Deucalion and progenitrix of the new race of men after the Flood.

† The following astonishing blasphemy may be found on p. 53, 4th Woman's-Rights Convention, in a speech of Mrs. H. B. Black-

Nor vaunt your victories o'er the host
Of Phlegra, in the Giants' war,
Inglorious fields, fought long ago
In Greece,—for Woman is your foe.

XCII.

When science shall have fledged her wings
Woman shall drive you from your place,
And purge the old, and build new things,
And found fresh empires for our race;
All that the farthest planet rings
Is ours, and all our system's space,
And on, if any central sun
The ecliptic of our centre run.

XCIII.

"But come, and would ye prove our might,
Since vain is ambush and surprise,
Descend to-morrow by moonlight;
We to the middle airs will rise.
There will we battle for our Right:
The Moon shall be the victor's prize;
But let that army which shall lose
Cease to be thenceforth Gods or Blues."

---

well, U. S. : " I expect some day to become greater than my present conceptions of my Creator. I expect to climb the mountains continually, onward and heavenward for ever."

" If," says the same lady, "Immortality means anything, it means unceasing Progress for the Individual and the Race."

XCIV.

She said: her Thought flew swift as light;
The winged Words that spurned the ground
Sprang after; up the airy height
Wave after wave propelled the sound;
Soon, like spent swimmers through the night,
Faintly they neared the vast profound,
Paused on the verge—then, shivering, crossed,
And sank, in Space and Silence lost.

BOOK IV.

ARGUMENT.

CORNELIA'S Thought, arriving in the Moon, delivers her challenge to the Gods, who sit in silence and fear, till Memory, casting her charm over their hearts, arouses a vision of the past, and brings in masque across the stage Reverence, Monarchy, Loyalty and Poetry, after which, on the exhortation of Juno, they arm for battle, and their arms are described. Venus seeks Vulcan in Etna and begs from him an enchanted shield, and he, complying, makes for her the shield of Vanity, which is described. The women on the other side being equipped for battle, mount into the air by moonlight, leaving Amadis and Celia bound upon earth to be sacrificed on their return after victory. In the air they are met by the Gods, led by Apollo, who sings like a minstrel part of the song of Demodocus, and challenges the women to match him. He is answered by Pastorella, who sings of Marriage in a pre-diluvian epic, which fills him with rage and despair, and drives him back into the silence of the Moon. On the flight of Apollo, the maids advancing to battle, Pyrrha is killed by Artemis, while, on the other side, Love is put to flight by Sibylla. The Gods discharge their arrows at the women, who, protected in their flying turrets, receive them with indifference, and assail the Gods with all the newly-invented missiles of modern science, and at last put them to flight. While the women are in full pursuit, and chanting a Pæan of Progress, Venus flies to the rear, and uncovers the shield of Vanity, by which she draws up the women to the extreme verge of the air, and then leaves them to fall into Infinite Space. The Poem is concluded by an address of Venus to the women who still remain upon earth.

BOOK IV.

I.

MEANTIME the Thought pursued her way,
Freed from the shadow of the Earth,
Shooting along the Sun's bright ray
To the Moon's Paradise of Mirth;
Then moved in silence through her play,
Well-buskined, conscious of her worth,
And cast, regardless of the odds,
Cornelia's cartel to the Gods.

II.

Still sat the Gods, and laughed no more;
Cold were their hearts, their eyes were wan;
So heavy seemed the times and hoar:
They thought on glories old and gone,
Their shrines unroofed by many a shore,
Fair Pæstum's piles and Parthenon,
And marble lives by Phidias formed,
And walls Apelles' colours warmed.

III.

Then, in their midst, rose Memory sage,
And o'er their hearts a glamour cast,
Waking the melodies of age,
As Dawn wakes Memnon in the waste;
And on the empty silent stage
They saw the spectres of the Past,
And in their eyes immortal tears
Shone, and remembrance of the years.

IV.

For as the towns, high citadelled,
And monarchs, warriors, statesmen, rose,
Once more they felt the airs of Eld,
And breathed again the Olympian snows;
Men in their markets they beheld;
Man's laughter and the sound of woes
They heard; but when these Forms were past,
Four more celestial came the last.

V.

First Reverence, with her garments rent;
Pensive she stood, as one who dreamed,
Her face upon her bosom bent;
A broken Image she'd redeemed
From earth, and on an altar leant,
Veiling her eyes, and so, it seemed,
Sought in her breast the sacred ray,
Once found in Heaven,—then passed away.

VI.

And after her came Monarchy,
Whom dwarfs, low lovers of the ground,
By Envy's counsel given, lest he
Should top their level, had discrowned.
Besides, his hands, though seeming free,
Invisibly with gold were bound.
He in the midst, like palest ghost,
Paused, hovered, lingered,—and was lost.

VII.

Next Loyalty, and on her breast
The dying Advocate she bore;
His lips the holy chalice pressed;
His life seemed ebbing from its shore;
Yet his weak hand his liege confessed;
His eyes his master's wrongs deplore.
So, with his King's name on his breath,
Loyalty with Berryer yields to Death.*

VIII.

But Poetry the last drew near
With Homer's harp-strings half in rust;
Yet to the earth she bent her ear,
And in her eyes shone hope, in trust

---

* See the letter written by M. Berryer on his death-bed to the Comte de Chambord, and published in *The Times*, December 10, 1868:—
"O Monseigneur, O mon Roi, on me dit que je touche à ma dernière heure. Je meurs avec la douleur de n'avoir pas vu le triomphe de vos

That songs of genius still were clear;
Clear rose a song,—the song was Lust;
Her strings she rent, and o'er her head
Tossing wild arms, for ever fled.

IX.

So passed the Masque in silent show;
And afterwards the Gods sat dumb;
Nor any laughed, but leaned his brow
Dreaming upon his palm, for some
Pondered the Past, and some the Now,
And others the far Time to come.
Then Juno speaks: still thunder rolls,
And breaks the silence in their souls.

X.

"Three cities were to me most dear,*
Mycene of the ample way,
Argos, and Sparta, cities clear
In song and memory,—where are they?

---

droits héréditaires, consacrant l'établissement et le developpement des libertés dont notre patrie a besoin.

"Je porte ces vœux au ciel pour votre Majesté, pour sa Majesté la Reine, pour notre chère France, pour qu'ils soient moins indignes d'être exaucés par Dieu. Je quitte la vie armé de tous les secours de notre sainte religion. Adieu, sire. Que Dieu vous protège et sauve la France.

"Votre dévoué et fidèle sujet,
"BERRYER."

* " Τὸν δ' ἠμείβετ' ἔπειτα βοῶπις πότνια Ἥρη·
Ἤτοι ἐμοὶ τρεῖς μὲν πολὺ φίλταραί εἰσι πόληες,
Ἄργος τε Σπάρτη τε καὶ εὐρυάγυια Μυκήνη."
HOM.: *Il.* iv. 52.

These twenty centuries the dumb steer
Turns to the plough their ashes grey:
Time that has made my cities clods
Now shakes his terrors at their gods.

XI.

"But if the Soul be lord of Time,
And we that move it grow not old,
This day shall prove;—for in the prime
Did Juno rule o'er woman hold;
All ye o'er passions set sublime
Were kings; now arm ye and be bold;
And show these maids that we, though driven
From Earth, are still high Gods in Heaven."

XII.

Then she her brow with dreadful look
Crowned with the Graces and the Hours,*
Her golden staff and cuckoo took,
And bright pomegranate, fruit and flowers,
And queenlike o'er her shoulder shook
Her veil in gleaming silvery showers,
Bright emblem of connubial law
To Gods, to mortal women awe.

---

* These and what follow were the emblems of Hera. See SMITH's *Dictionary of Antiquities*, under her name.

XIII.

Then silent and august around
In majesty the Gods arose;
Jove's brow once more the Seasons crowned
With circling rains, flowers, fruits, and snows.
There stood the shaker of the ground,
Neptune; and she who makes men foes,
Bellona, scourge of bright corn-land;
And mail-clad Mars, with Scythian brand.

XIV.

But Pallas, daughter of high Jove,*
Dropt on the threshold of her sire
The raiment her own hands had wove,
Her broidered beautiful attire,
And clasping on her limbs above
Jove's tunic, armed for battle dire;
Her ægis from her shoulder hung
Deep fringed, and dreadful splendours flung.

XV.

For it is compassed all with Dread;
Strife, Strength, and the Ice-fear of Pursuit
Are on it, and the Gorgon's head,
Jove's portent, terrible and brute;

---

* " Αὐτὰρ 'Αθηναίη κούρη Διὸς αἰγιόχοιο
Πέπλον μὲν κατέχευεν ἑανὸν πατρὸς ἐπ' οὔδει
Ποίκιλον, ὅν ῥ' αὐτὴ ποιήσατο καὶ κάμε χέρσιν.
Ἡ δὲ χιτῶν' ἐνδῦσα Διὸς νεφεληγερέταο
Τεύχεσιν ἐς πόλεμον θωρήσσετο δακρυόεντα.
'Αμφὶ δ' ἄρ' ὤμοισιν βάλετ' αἰγίδα θυσσανόεσσαν,

Her helmet, from whose cone outspread
Her crests four ways diverging shoot,
Is gold : beneath the enormous plume
A hundred cities might find room.

XVI.

With silver shafts, whose deathly hiss
The Python heard, and sweetest lyre,
Apollo came ; and Artemis,
Whose feet no sylvan stag can tire ;
Arrows she bore of bitter bliss,
Whence love-lorn maids their death desire ;
Lit by her torch-light, silvery, wan,
On her veiled brow the crescent shone.

XVII.

And Mercury, well skilled to swim
Over the void and airless deep :
Him his winged cap and sandals trim—
Beautiful, golden—buoyant keep.
A staff he carries, to make dim
The eyes of men, and break their sleep ;
And herewith hopes he soon to guide
The souls of Maids o'er Lethe's tide.

Δεινὴν, ἥν περὶ μὲν πάντη φόβος ἐστεφάνωται,
Ἐν δ' Ἔρις, ἐν δ' Ἀλκή, ἐν δὲ κρυόεσσα Ἰωκή,
Ἐν δέ τε Γοργείη κεφαλὴ δεινοῖο πελώρου,
Δεινή τε, σμερδνή τε, Διὸς τέρας αἰγιόχοιο·
Κρατὶ δ' ἐπ' ἀμφίφαλον κυνέην θέτο τετραφάληρον
Χρυσείην, ἑκατὸν πολίων πρυλέεσσ' ἀραρυῖαν."

Hom.: *Il.* v. 733.

XVIII.

But ere the night of battle came,
Venus, advising with her heart,
(For she of all the Gods, through shame,
Dreaded the most Cornelia's art),
For fear lest Science and the Dame
Prevail o'er Heavenly shield and dart,
Sought Vulcan—who, for all her Gretna
Green trips, continued kind—in Etna.

XIX.

Vulcan had mounted with his choir,
And through the Moon's Volcanoes strayed,
And gauged them; but not finding fire,
He doubted long 'twixt Love and Trade;
Then, when the flame of his desire
Proved weaker, business he obeyed;
And him his gold-haired wife now found
In his old Smithy underground.

XX.

But here, where once the Cyclops swinked
Had laboured, all was dark, the bellows
Unblown, the furnace half extinct,
Hammer and tongs no more were fellows;
Low embers by the caldron winked,
And showed the God, who, once so jealous,
The husband vigilant to boring,
Slept cross-legged, most distinctly snoring.

XXI.

The Goddess at her partner's side
   Stood gazing on his grimy features,
Then, tapping his broad shoulder, cried,
"Wake, best and sleepiest of all creatures!
   Why in such sloth do you abide?
   For surely, since the shower of meteors,
You've stuff to busy as your wont is
Pyracmon, Steropes, and Brontes.

XXII.

"Since your dear stepson's arms were made
   (Though every day I get fresh scars),
Not once, my pet,* I've tasked your trade
   To equip me for my woman's wars.
   Now peril dire demands your aid,
   For impious Woman climbs the Stars;
Our Moon's at stake, and Heaven must yield,
Save you'll vouchsafe me magic shield.

XXIII.

"For in some wondrous armour dight
   Her heart invulnerable seems:
Love hath she worsted in fair fight,
   And balked wise Momus' secret dreams;

---

* See the pretty womanly coaxing by which Venus in *Æneid.* 8, 370, gets Vulcan to make the shield of Æneas. The "carissime conjux" in the face of the song of Demodocus in the *Odyssey* is very charming.

Now Science would our deeds requite,
And we, reduced to worst extremes,
Our armies from the Earth driv'n back,
Expect in Heaven the last attack.

XXIV.

" But thou, Artificer, whose care
Once forged Heaven's bolts, in massy mould,
Some wondrous metal now prepare,
Stronger than copper, brass, or gold ;
Hence beat a target that shall bear
Each fierce assault of woman bold,
And Science, emptying all her train
Of red artillery, smite in vain."

XXV.

The God replied : " My dearest Life,
Not often do you make the stages
To these dull Isles, albeit my wife;
Else had you known that now for ages
I and my workmen are at strife,
Who, thinking scorn of my just wages,
Have started in Vesuvius' gorge
A vast co-operative forge.

XXVI.

" And I, who thought the whole concern
Was bound to perish soon or later,
For want of Capital, now learn
They've lately started a new crater.

But to this question to return,—
To forge a shield's a weighty matter!
But still, to save the Moon and you,
I'll try what Vulcan yet can do."

XXVII.

He said, and raised the bellows vast;
Up sprang the flames, and roared, and spread;
Catania trembled in the blast;
Messina's Straits were all blood-red;
Northwards the fierce refulgence passed
To Naples; shone Palermo's Head;
And east the Ionian sea-beat caves
Gleamed; and round Malta gleamed the waves.

XXVIII.

The hammer fell, the sparkles flew,
The caldron hissed, and in the heat
The God's stiff limbs all supple grew,
And merrily on the forge he beat,
He hit so timely and so true,
That soon his labour was complete;
And he to her pleased eyes revealed
The bright, full-orbed, enchanted Shield.

XXIX.

The oval orb, that every limb
Concealed, of purest crystal made,
Was featly bound in silver rim;
And on the rim the Smith essayed

(For History was well known to him,
Beyond the custom of his trade)
In sculptured signs to carve and chase
The Fortunes of the Female Race.

XXX.

High over all sat Womanhood,
Who from a love-tale on the lute
Had paused awhile; and round her stood
The Passions, mingled in dispute;
Each over other, as he could,
Desired her favour for his suit;
She in the midst misdoubting sat,
With troubled looks this way and that.

XXXI.

For Reason moved her on the right,
And him, methinks, she fain had heard;
But Love and Hope in her despite
Upon the left her bosom stirred;
And Vanity, as colours bright
Betray the oft-bewildered bird,
Brought her fair gifts, which through her eyes
Turned her light hearing from the wise.

XXXII.

Beneath, he made with wondrous art
Pandora through the crevice peer;
And to her face did so impart
In medley fancy, hope, and fear,

You felt the fluttering of her heart
Beneath the silver, and could hear
The foolish breath, that came unbid,
And went; nor had she raised the lid.

XXXIII.

Next Bluebeard's wife, condemned to die,
Calls to her tyrant from her knees,
And, whilst the desperate minutes fly,
Entreats, yet seems not to appease.
One hand his sabre whirls on high,
The other shows the bloody keys.
Above, with eyes that strain to scan
The cruel distance—Sister Anne.

XXXIV.

And histories there were shown beside
Of Atalanta's doleful case,
By three fair apples drawn aside
To lose her freedom with the race;
And of Tarpeia old, who died
Through Vanity, a traitress base;
And Scylla, for one fierce, brief night,
Her father's slayer, her city's blight.

XXXV.

Now on the side opposing this,
Four Queens were made, to show what Power
To woman does: Semiramis
Her husband slew, to build a tower;

And there, with lips all warm to kiss,
The Egyptian Queen dissolved her dower,
And, floating 'neath her silken dome,
Fanned half the manhood out of Rome.

XXXVI.

Next, scourge of Spain, Elizabeth,
And Queen of twice a thousand gowns,*
At seventy leads the dance of death,†
Wearing false hair 'neath England's crowns ; ‡
Her Heralds call with windy breath
Each loyal Apelles of her towns
To adore Campaspe, and to save
Black teeth and wrinkles from the grave. §

XXXVII.

The last great Catherine, for the dead
Still wearing bloody widow's weeds ;
Her starving peasants bring her bread
Whence she her boorish lovers feeds :

---

* The number found in Elizabeth's wardrobe after her death.

† She danced with the Duke of Nevers at the age of sixty-nine. "She courted hym in the best manner ; he, on the other syde, used many compliments, as kissing her hand, yea, and her foote, when she showed him her legg."

‡ "She wore false hair of a red colour, surmounted by a crown of gold."—*Lingard*, vol. vi. p. 654.

§ Elizabeth, by proclamation, announced to her people that none of the portraits which had hitherto been taken of her person did justice to the original, and that, at the request of her Council, she had resolved to procure an exact likeness from the pencil of some able artist.—*Lingard*, vol. vi. p. 657.

These round her sit ; the board is spread ;
Sweet music sounds ; she little heeds,
Pleased with the pictured wall that shows
Sacked Ismail and her slaughtered foes.*

XXXVIII.

Now neither of those shields that won
For our Prince Arthur fame in fight,†
Or Spanish Roger, matched this one
(The Shield of Vanity it hight):
Theirs made indeed the foemen run,
But this if any mortal wight
Beheld, unclouded by its case,
He gazed till Domesday in its face.

XXXIX.

But him no Gorgon horror froze ;
In that broad mirror pride and pique
Are soothed ; here every vulture nose
Looks Roman ; every snub is Greek ;
No wart nor pimple ever shows,
But soft carnation dyes each cheek ;
To Nireus turns Thersites base,
And hag Canidia seems a Grace.

---

* It is said that Catherine was strangely insensible to music, and used, when at dinner, to feast her eyes on the two pictures by Cazenova of the sack of Otchakoff and Ismail, in which he "represented with hideous accuracy the blood flowing in streams, the limbs torn from the body and still palpitating, the demoniac fury of the slaughterers, and the convulsive agonies of the slaughtered."—*Tooke's Life of Catherine II.*

† See *Faery Queen*, 5, 8, 37, 38.

XL.

Meantime, while thus the Lemnian sire
Was travailing with fire and wind,
The warlike Maids their heads attire,
Their breasts with plates of velvet bind,
String their light bows for battle dire,
Their quivers fill, their arrows grind,
Which oft in peaceful strife have sped
To heart of bull's-eye or of red.

XLI.

And deadly engines they prepare
For airy battle, passing count,
War's dire inventions, new and rare;
Mortars and howitzers they mount,
Swift-shooting needle-guns they bear,
And rockets pile a fiery fount,
And shells by cunning science made
To burst in air, and swift grenade.

XLII.

All for high travel are equipped
By aid of Science ; some assume
Wings like a swallow, arrow-tipt,
Glossy and smooth, with purple bloom ;
One soars through air securely shipt,
Arion-like, on magic broom,
Of all her sticks—so said the vendor—
Once loveliest to the Witch of Endor.

XLIII.

Some in swift barks, concealed from sight
'Neath cupolas, are drawn along,
Vessels than gossamer more light,
But yet as heaviest iron strong,
Tugged up by many a soaring kite,
Like old Chineses in Hong Kong;
Each tower has air-holes like a flute,
Through which their balls they safely shoot.

XLIV.

Some in balloon-like airy barge,
Governed by many a dexterous oar,
Prepare swift needles to discharge;
Some upon huge Steam-Dragons soar,
Bearing for shield a seven-fold targe,
With iron plated to the core;
And at her waist, the host to light,
Each bears a silver lantern bright.

XLV.

But while with armaments so vast
The College precincts all resound,
Poor Amadis lies prisoned fast,
With Celia in vile durance bound;
These two, in fiery holocaust,
Cornelia, soon with conquest crowned,
Intends to sacrifice, a high
Thanksgiving for her victory.

XLVI.

Then gentle dames (if there be those
Still left unto our brawling time,
Who love kind Nature and Repose,
Nor judge man's Fancy to be crime)
Who with the reddening of the rose,
Day-dreamers in romance or rhyme,
Dare still indulge your summer sense
In Castles of sweet Indolence;

XLVII.

Who, yet to public warfare strange,
Where men must push, and lie, and thieve,
Live, and, unconscious of all change,
Your own sweet Instinct still believe,
Who, with more large and human range,
As Nature bids you, love and grieve,
And signify your sovereign will
To save the world its women still;

XLVIII.

If on the inhospitable earth
Ophelia's meekness still find place;
If Beatrice's maiden mirth,
And Portia's wit, one woman grace;
If any maid of modern birth
Be piteous of thy cruel case,
Viola, or thine, best loved by men,
Thou queen of lovers, Imogen;

XLIX.

If such there be, now in attires
Of grief, and weeds that mourners use,
With long processions and sad choirs,
Let them approach the imperial Muse;
And at her altar breathe desires,
And vows, and prayers, that are her dues,
And for the happier estate,
Of these two lovers supplicate.

L.

Upon your knees, ye ladies, fall,
Be ye fresh maids, or wedded wives!
And low, at Love's confessional,
Where he your past transgressions shrives,
Vow, as the price of ransom, all
The meek obedience of your lives;
So Love, that hath the Muse's ear,
Haply your penitence shall hear.

LI.

Attend! As when by besom stirred,
The rising dust in sunshine floats,
And all the slanting rays are blurred
With glittering dances; soon the motes
Vanish: so at the given word,
Wings, cars, and cupolas, and boats,
Together rose, and in moonlight
Passed brightly lessening out of sight.

LII.

Now in mid air the Maids behold,
Down shooting on the slant moonbeams,
The embattled Deities of old,
Lords of men's Passions and their Dreams ;
Immortal arms their limbs enfold,
Ambrosial radiance round them streams :
So once they passed in youth and joy
To battle on the plains of Troy.

LIII.

Of whom the foremost and most fair,
Like minstrel knight, Apollo sprang ;
All round him danced his dazzling hair
In moonshine, and his harp-strings rang :
Then trembled the terrestrial air,
For Love, and War, and Death, he sang ;
Hushed stood the night ; the rhythmic spheres
Rang with the songs of elder years.

LIV.

Memory unbarred the Muse's gate,
And loud he smote his harp-strings seven,
Singing the glories of the great,*
The song whose glory compassed Heaven,

---

* This is the subject of the old, the heroic, the barbarous :

" Μοῦς' ἄρ' ἀοιδὸν ἀνῆκεν ἀειδέμεναι κλέα ἀνδρῶν,
οἴμης, τῆς τότ' ἄρα κλέος οὐρανὸν εὐρὺν ἵκανεν,
νεῖκος Ὀδυσσῆος καὶ Πηλείδεω Ἀχιλῆος,
ὥς ποτε δηρίσαντο θεῶν ἐν δαιτὶ θαλείῃ

How once Odysseus moved by hate,
Had with the Son of Peleus striven,
And at the Immortals' plenteous board
Hot words provoked the warriors' sword:

LV.

And how the ruler of the host
Joyed that the bravest of the brave
Thus strove, remembering what accost
The God in divine Delphi gave,
When he the stony threshold crossed,
Apollo's oracle to crave;
And hence for Greek and Trojan rose,
So willed high Heaven, the fount of woes.

LVI.

Then pausing he the Maids bespoke—
"O women, whom high sense of worth,
And Titan Progress, thus provoke
To dare in fight celestial birth,
Now, if your Deity has woke
New moods of minstrelsy on earth,
Match me, I pray, with modern tune
This music of the ruder Moon."

ἐκπάγλοις ἐπέεσσιν, ἄναξ δ' ἀνδρῶν Ἀγαμέμνων
χαῖρε νόῳ, ὅτ' ἄριστοι Ἀχαιῶν δηριόωντο.
ὣς γάρ οἱ χρείων μυθήσατο Φοῖβος Ἀπόλλων
Πυθοῖ ἐν ἠγαθέῃ, ὅθ' ὑπέρβη λάϊνον οὐδὸν
χρησόμενος· τότε γάρ ῥα κυλίνδετο πήματος ἀρχὴ
Τρωσί τε καὶ Δαναοῖσι Διὸς μεγάλου διὰ βουλάς."

Hom.: *Odyssey*, 8. 73.

LVII.

Then forward flew the pensive Maid,
Fair Pastorelle, skilled on flute or fiddle
To sing to Shepherds in the shade,
And all their rustic doubts to unriddle;
Of Marriage much her pipe had played,
Faith, Duty, Passions of the Idyll,
Or such as his high strings arouse
Who sang "the Angel in the House."

LVIII.

Now on her winged steed full trot
She mounts to Heaven, nor fears to fall,
(Her steed swift Pegasus begot,
Strayed sometime to a Rector's stall),
Singing the hard but human lot,
That waits on wedded curates all.*
Mute hung both armies in the air,
These triumph fills, and these despair.

---

* These are the subjects chosen by the new, the pastoral, the progressive.
"Then the girl in her first youth
 Married a curate—handsome, poor in purse,
 Of gentle blood and manners, and he lived
 Under her father's roof as they had planned.
 Full soon, for happy years are short, they filled
 The house with children."
—*Laurance.* By JEAN INGELOW.

LIX.

And next she sang of wedded life
Before the Dodo and the Moa,
Japhet's mésalliance, and his wife,
And what Niloyah said to Noah;*
At last—to close the doubtful strife,
And prove that, in the modern Stoa,
Men even with their own wives may dwell
Resigned—she sang the letter L.†

---

* This is the manner in which the "Revolution" School of Poets opens an epic:—

> "Niloyah said to Noah, 'What aileth thee,
>   My master, unto whom is my desire,
>   The father of my sons?' He answered her,
> 'Mother of many children, I have heard
>   The voice again.' 'Ah me!' she saith, 'Ah me!
>   What spake it?' and with that Niloyah sighed."
>
> —*Story of Doom.*

† This is how modern Virtue writes of marriage. (N.B.—The "bold brown woman" is an old love of the husband).—

> "'My wife, how beautiful you are!'
>   Then closer at her side reclined.
> 'The bold brown woman from afar
>   Comes to me blind.
> And by comparison I see
>   The majesty of matron grace,
> And learn how pure, how fair can be
>   My own wife's face.'"
>
> —*The Letter L.*

A logical husband, indeed! who cannot feel sure of his own wife's purity and beauty, till he has applied what Mr. Mill calls the Method of Difference.

LX.

Rage seized the God, despair, and dread;
His harp fell shivering to the ground;
Swift turned he, and, with wings outspread,
Shot, lightning, to the vast profound;
Then, crossing, to the Moon he fled,
And sat in wrath, till, safe from sound,
Sweet Silence o'er his senses stole,
And healed the discord in his soul.

LXI.

But in the fight no pause there is,
On rush the Maids, fierce Pyrrha first:
At whom shot Love; nor did he miss,
The barb her heart-strings seemed to burst:
Yet still she raged: then Artemis,
Seeing her now for death athirst,
Sent, in great pity of her pain,
A sweet sharp arrow to her brain.

LXII.

Then down upon her shoulder she
Drooped her low head so sweetly slain,
As tired poppy heads you see
Bowed in the burden of much rain.*

---

* "Lassove papavera collo
Demisere caput, pluviâ quum forte gravantur."
VIRG.: *Æneid,* 9. 436.

Light Lesbia, weeping Lalage,
Their sister's quiet limbs sustain,
And took and bore her gently down,
Like Sleep and Death, to her own town. *

LXIII.

Love, who had thought the shaft his own,
Swiftly the airy champaign trod
Pursuing ; but his form was known :
The Sibyl seized the bloody rod :
Forth sprang she, daring all alone
The immortal Babe : then feared the God ;
Swift towards the stars his flight he wings,
And close behind Sibylla springs.

LXIV.

Then through the bosom of the night
Pell-mell the adverse missiles poured.
Do thou the fortunes of the fight,
Urania, heavenly Muse, record,
Deeds done beyond my mortal sight,
Where never hawk nor heron soared,
Nor bold discoverer of the sky,
Save English Astulph, dared to fly.

---

* See the passage in the *Iliad*, where Sleep and Death carry the body of Sarpedon back to Lycia.

LXV.

First on the Maids fierce arrows fell,
Sharp, swift, and slant, like silver rain,
Such as in other times men tell
Stymphalus' cursed brood had slain,
Or sweet Alcestis saved from hell,
Or pierced Orion in the main ;
Then Mars' bright spear, with vengeance hurled,
Reddened the stars, and shook the world.

LXVI.

But safely housed their ships within,
And walls by Science triply steeled,
The women let them smite and spin,
On tower, and targe, and plated shield ;
They cared no more to hear the din,
Than when the snow-winds from the field
Beat the warm roofs in idle ire,
Where Yule-tide gossips mend the fire.

LXVII.

At once, in every iron grot,
The gunners their fusees prepare,
Then, in an instant, fire and shot
Burn into red the blazing air ;
Myriads of needles mount red-hot ;
Swift flights of flaming arrows glare ;
A thousand rockets curve their road
In fire ; a thousand bombs explode.

LXVIII.

Incessantly the radiance red
Flames, and incessantly expires;
The air, driven in by impulse dread,
Plunged backwards, as the sea retires
In earthquake huge; you might have said
A million meteoric fires,
Wild off-cast of a million suns,
Had burst upon our world at once.

LXIX.

Oft plunged as in some airy grave,
The women sank in sudden void;
As sudden with resurgent wave
Shot starwards, on the summit buoyed;
But little feared those Sailors brave,
Nay, rather in the peril joyed;
Featly they tack, unreef, or furl,
And still their red artillery hurl.

LXX.

But vain beneath that iron hail
Was all the armoury of Heaven;
Now riven is Mars' bright coat of mail,
Medusa's marble head is riven;
Cold as the surges in a gale,
The ichor round their hearts is driven;
And long to silence used, new fears
Break in with thunder through their ears.

LXXI.

Once more it seemed their giant foes,
Upheaving their incumbent piles,
Typhon in flames of Etna rose,
Enceladus with all his isles,
Straining with supreme spasm to close
In thunder on their doomed files:
Ruin and Rout before them spread
Their hideous shapes: they turned and fled.

LXXII.

Then, drunk with hope and fierce delight,
The women, freed from mortal awe,
Forgot the limits of their flight,
And empty space and nature's law;
Above them shone the boundless night;
The rolling planet-worlds they saw,
Their destined realms;—and as they sprang
In swift pursuit the army sang:

LXXIII.

"The Gods are fled! The Gods are fled!
The film is fallen from our eyes!
The heart is vanquished by the head!
Ho! for the secrets of the skies!
Now the world's ocean all outspread
Waits for the traffic of the wise:
Nor fear nor death our passage bars;
We mount for ever to the stars.

LXXIV.

"Ye planets! whom on Ida's hill,
  Or on the lone Chaldæan lawn,
The shepherd loved with Gods to fill,
  Mercury, at set of sun withdrawn,
And Venus, beautiful and still,
  White empress of the dewy dawn;
To whom, with altars on the sward,
He bowed in weakness, and adored;

LXXV.

" Bright lamps! whom once with childish fears
  We watched ascending from your caves,
Steering through all the tangled spheres,
  Or rolling westward to the waves;
How still, how godlike, clad in years,
  Ye gleamed above our fathers' graves!
But now hath Science broke the pale.
Your Gods are fled! Ye planets, hail!

LXXVI.

"Mount, mount, O Women, mount! For us
  Life has no bounds, and Hope no goals.
Thus soar we to the Moon, and thus
  Shall seek from thence the snowy poles
Of Mars, and yet where Uranus,
  Or where extremest Neptune rolls,
Or lodged with Saturn shall see clear
His moons, and rings and endless year.

LXXVII.

"And when those silent worlds we reach,
If they be tenantless, new springs
Of art shall rise, and human speech :
Or, haply, on Discovery's wings,
We may find some slave-star to teach
Our Freedom and contempt of kings ;
And Heaven shall breathe from fire to fire
Our harmonies, one living lyre.

LXXVIII.

" Bright Hope! What deserts shall we till !
To what poor captives bring release !
Time shall his cycles there fulfill
With Innocence and dove-like Peace.
There Hate and Envy, Wrath and Ill,
Shall perish, and all Pride shall cease ;
Yet shall Equality secure
The rich, for none shall then be poor.

LXXIX.

" Death's self, who now makes mortals bend,
Strong man and weak, young maid and hoar,
Tears child from sire, and friend from friend,
Shall visit those bright worlds no more ;
There new electric fires shall lend
Their succours, and our veins restore ;
New herbs recruit life's sinking wave ;
New minerals cheat the expectant grave.

LXXX.

" Therefore farewell to thee, O Earth,
  With all thy passion, strife, and pain,
  Thy dark extremes of dower and dearth,
  Outwearied land, and toiling main!
  Let those who now desire new birth,
  Mount, and experience Woman's reign.
  Now the new Dawn her light hath shed!
  The Heavens are free! The Gods are fled!" *

LXXXI.

Thus they: but far from shot and spear,
Venus had watched the doubtful field;
Now sprang she to the flying rear,
And her broad crystal orb revealed;
Full on it smote the moonbeams clear;
Then radiant shone the enchanted shield,
As the reflector far and wide
Shoots the lamp's radiance o'er the tide.

---

* Some will, doubtless, object that generous sentiments are deserving of praise rather than punishment. Yet it is somewhat mortifying to our vanity to remember that philanthropic talk of this kind was, before the French Revolution, common in the mouths of men who, in a few years' time, were drinking each other's blood, or superintending the Noyades. It was once the opinion of Jeremiah that "the heart is deceitful above all things, and desperately wicked." Since the French Revolution *nous avons changé tout cela*. "This very afternoon," says a female philosopher of the States, "I heard quoted in the Temperance Convention—but there is no such passage in the Bible—' the heart of man is prone to evil, and that continually.' Now *we* know that man is prone to good, and that continually. So thoroughly good is human nature, that, in spite of bad laws, man is not so bad as he might be under them."—*Report of Fourth Woman's-Rights Convention, p.* 66.

LXXXII.

Straight as the needle seeks its star,
And swift as steel to magnet draws,
Around the wondrous Shield from far,
Obedient to celestial laws,
The Maidens came; the airy war
They quite forgot, forgot their cause;
For lost in vanity, poor elves!
They saw but their own beauteous selves.

LXXXIII.

The Goddess paused one moment dread,
Then slow, sublime, begins to rise,
And, as some comet, fiery, red,
Flames on the nations by surprise,
And with its monstrous tail outspread
Mounts sunwards, grasping all the skies;
And men grow pale beneath the stars,
Dreaming of earthquakes, plagues, and wars;

LXXXIV.

So now the Immortals far beneath
Behold the Maids drawn up on high,
Following the Shield with bated breath,
Mechanic oar, and stony eye;
Thus Mercury's staff o'er streams of Death
Conducts the souls of those who die;
Now grows earth's breath more fine and rare;
They reach the limits of the air.

LXXXV.

First to the verge the Goddess came,
And crossed it: in the Sun's bright rays
The burning crystal seemed aflame,
Shrivelling their eyeballs in its blaze;
Yet still the Maids, with faint blind aim,
As fluttering moths whom candles daze,
Flew onwards, reached the farthest bound,
Passed it, then sank in the Profound.

LXXXVI.

But steadfast on the airy ball
Holding aloof her crystal wonder,
Up-towered the Queen majestical,
And rolled to earth a voice like thunder:
"Matrons, and Maids, and Women all,
Who worship Heaven, and dwell thereunder,
Still honouring Eld, nor seek to unsphere
Custom and Sex, attend and fear!

LXXXVII.

"I, Venus, of the charmèd zone,
Child of the fresh foam of the Sea,
Had chosen woman as mine own,
For fairest of fair things was she;
Perfected Grace was hers alone;
Her limbs I made more delicately;
She ruled by soft Persuasion's charms;
And Wit and Weakness were her arms.

LXXXVIII.

"And loyal Devotion crowned her brows,
    Eager to give and slow to seek;
Enough it seemed to rule man's house,
    Silent and beautiful and meek;
Fair Modesty had all her vows;
    Apt scholar of the noblest Greek,*
In haunts of men unseen, unheard,
She her sweet privacy preferred.

LXXXIX.

" So when the blood-red star malign
    Rose, and wild Revolution's blast
Shook all things ancient or divine,
    When every fool blasphemed the Past,
Yet woman watched the sacred shrine,
    And held her olden anchors fast,
As through fire, earthquake, storm, eclipse,
Tranquilly ride the harboured ships.

---

* See the Funeral Oration of Pericles :—

"εἰ δέ με δεῖ καὶ γυναικειάς τι ἀρετῆς, ὅσαι νῦν ἐν χηρείᾳ ἔσονται, μνησθῆναι, βραχείᾳ παραινέσει ἅπαν σημανῶ· τῆς τε γὰρ ὑπαρχούσης φύσεως μὴ χείροσι γενέσθαι ὑμῖν μεγάλη ἡ δόξα, καὶ ἧς ἂν ἐπ' ἐλάχιστον ἀρετῆς πέρι ἢ ψόγου ἐν τοῖς ἄρσεσι κλέος ᾖ."

THUCYDIDES: Book ii. 45.

"If I must say something about the excellence of women also—such as may now be in widowhood—I will signify it all in brief advice. For not to fall below the nature that you already have, is your great glory, and hers, too, is great glory, whose name is least often heard in men's mouths, either for good or for evil."

XC.

"Nay, like the drifting vessel's chart,
  She taught mankind the sands to shun;
And mother's milk did Truth impart,
  And sisters' lives to Honour won;
For who, that's felt a mother's heart,
Can be an all degenerate son?*
And who, that knows a sister's name
Means Loyalty, be deaf to Shame?

XCI.

"The sick man's brow and labouring breath
  Grew easier when her form passed by;
Her image in the hour of death
  Last faded from the clouding eye;
Nay, oft she seemed to man beneath
A hope of Immortality,
Else Pity, Charity, and Trust,
Angels of Heaven, were counted dust.

---

* This is not at all the light in which the votaries of Social Science regard their mothers. In an able paper read last year, Mr. Myers is reported to have said, "Motherhood, at least, was within woman's sphere; and was the mother's influence—an educational engine to which all others were mere child's play—to be intrusted to designed incompetence and predetermined imbecility?"—*Report of National Association for Promoting Social Science*, 1868, *p*. 451. Have these educational engineers no perception of the meaning implied in our very expressive idiom "mother wit?"

XCII.

"Yet was she mortal and of earth;
One frailty to her soul I gave;
By Vanity I sealed her birth,
And now is Vanity her grave;
Ah, that one fault should cloud such worth!
Yet Virtue is too weak to save!
Nor Wit shall e'er outweigh the excess,
Nor Beauty nor Delightfulness.

XCIII.

"For once I gave from Heaven above,
To mother, daughter, sister, wife,
As chosen Priestesses of Love,
The sacred keys of Private Life;
This was my dear untrodden grove,*
Sheltered from storms of public strife,
Shaded from the eye of garish day,
Where myriad Fancies still might play.

XCIV.

"But some, by Vanity beguiled,
Threw wide my dark and quiet door,
And vulgar Pride, Ambition wild,
Rushed in, and Hatred, and Uproar;

---

* " τὰν ἄβατον θεοῦ
φυλλάδα, μυριόκαρπον, ἀνήλιον,
ἀνήνεμόν τε πάντων
χειμώνων."

SOPH.: Œ. C., 675.

And now my grove is all defiled,
There Peace and Fancy play no more;
Gone is the Illusion, and Life's bloom
Is lost.   Enough!   They have their doom.

XCV.

"Too weak their vanity to rein,
They soared, by Hope and Madness driven,
Heaven's starry Silence to profane,
And sinned the sin that's ne'er forgiven.
Now ye, who still on Earth remain,
Read well your hearts, and reverence Heaven;
Born to short years, hope not too high,
But live, remembering ye must die!"

XCVI.

She said: but as the Muses tell,
The Women, from the airy steep
Dashed headlong, fell, and fell, and fell,
From space to space, from deep to deep,
Through voids, where Death alone can dwell,
And Silence, and eternal Sleep;
Down, ever downwards, resting never,
They fell, and so shall fall for ever.

THE END.

www.ingramcontent.com/pod-product-compliance
Lightning Source LLC
Chambersburg PA
CBHW030309170426
43202CB00009B/936